Shungite Reality
a study of energy

N.L. Hopkins
in collaboration with
Walt Silva and Derek Condit

Edited by Jan Shaw

Copyright © 2019 N.L. Hopkins

All rights reserved.

ISBN: 9781706584483

Cover Bee Photo by Nowaja from Pixabay

DEDICATION

To those who seek the truth
and believe in a new reality,
The Shungite Grid Makers.

We can do this...

CONTENTS

	Dedication	I
	Preface	iv
1	**What is Shungite and what will it do for me?**	1
	Enerology	5
	The Quantum Field	6
	What Is Shungite?	6
	Where Is Shungite Found?	7
	Fullerene - C60 Molecule	8
	Shungite's C60	9
	Types of Shungite	10
	Shungite Test	11
	Shungite "Nuggets"	11
	Water Purification	12
	Shungite Energized Water vs Shungite Water	13
	Health Benefits	13
	Environmental Protection	15
	The Path Begins	15
	Electronic Warfare	18
	Shungite Science - Simplified	20
	Shungite Nuggets - Water	21
	Resonance	24
	Nuggets and Your Electric System	27
	Shungite Powder	29
	Shungite S4 Powder	32
	Shungite S4 Magnets	35
	Shungite and Efficiency	37
	Individual Protection - Pendants	40
2	**Customer Testimonials**	45
3	**Frequently Asked Questions**	113
4	**Enerology and Shungite Science**	163
	The Universe of Spiritual Intervention (USI)	163
	Vibrational Medicine	163
	Energy Healing	167
	Reiki, Acupuncture, Herbal, Homeopathy	167-169
	Sympathetic Resonance	169
	Energy Healing Devices	170
	Raymond Royal Rife (1888-1971)	172
	Dr. Wilhelm Reich (1897-1957)	174
	Why Keep it Secret?	175
	Enerology	180
	The Quantum Field	182
	Shungite Science	183
	Walt Silva	183
	Orgone Energy	184
	1. Shungite Accelerates Electric Signals and Orgone.	185
	2. Shungite Reverses Electric and Radio Waves.	187

	3. Toxic Molecules Fall Apart in a Shungite Energy Field.	189
	4. Secondary Electric Devices Need Shungite.	190
	5. With Shungite Small Is More Energetic.	190
	6. Silver Saturated Shungite Attenuates Wifi Signals.	191
	7. The C60 Fullerene Is the Secret Behind Shungite.	194
	"The Vector Equilibrium"	196
	8. Every Particle of Shungite Is Quantum Entangled.	198
	Quantum Entanglement	199
	9. Shungite C60 Is Superior to Lab Made C60.	202
	10. Shungite Loves Energy Fields.	210
	11. Shungite Creates Energy Savings.	206
	12. Three Pieces of Shungite Creates a Coherent Field.	206
	13. Shungite Promotes Healing.	208
	Gaia's Gift	212
	14. Shungite Energy Made for Specific Purposes.	219
	15. Does Shungite Have Sentience?	222
	The 5g Death March	225
5	**Shungite, the Bees and the Sixth Extinction Event**	227
	Derek Condit, the Bee Guy	227
	The Sixth Extinction	228
	Why Is Emf/wifi Radiation Damaging?	229
	Shungite and the Honeybees	236
	The Shungite Beehives	240
	Conclusion	241
	The Shungite World Grid	242
	How Do We Turn Around the 5g Death March	245
	Index	247

PREFACE

Welcome to the next episode in my life story. The previous episodes are contained in two separate books under the one cover of *Cosmic Reality* published in 2013. Since then, the rabbit hole took me on a journey into Shungite Reality. It led to the back door.

This is a book about Shungite, a black coal-like mineral found one place in the world - Russia. Edgar Cayce, arguably the most impressive psychic of the 20th Century, said, "...out of Russia comes again the hope of the world." And Shungite has given me the solid hope that what it teaches about its magical properties can assist humanity in coming of age. It is time to reclaim our position as caretakers of Earth.

While the book is written from my perspective, it could not have been written without input from Walt Silva and Derek Condit. I will present information based upon Walt's understanding of energy science and Derek's experiences establishing Shungite Beehives that inspired a worldwide reaction. Shungite Bees are showing us how to save the Honeybees and save ourselves.

My profound gratitude goes out to all those others who have participated in this Shungite Story, specifically those customers who took the time to add their testimonial. Rev. Lee Brown sent me on this journey by introducing me to Shungite. I would still be writing this book, if not for the assistance of Jan Shaw's insights and editing. Sofiya Blank's contribution of Kirlian photographs of Shungite are invaluable. Irma Simuni's translations of Russian facilitated critical communication between Sofiya, myself and Walt, and this book is being translated into Russian by Irma, as it has been written. Dolly Howard took the journey with me, every step of the way. I am profoundly grateful to you all.

Nancy Hopkins 11/24/19

Chapter 1

What is Shungite and what will it do for me?

So, you have picked up this book in search of answers regarding "Shungite". You have numerous questions and may find it hard to swallow all the hype about a rock. Well, more accurately, about a mineral mix that has a typical carbon base ranging from 35-98% carbon depending upon where the sample was mined. And where is it mined and did it really fall to Earth some 2.5 billion years ago? And can it actually purify water and soil; demonstrate healing capabilities; protect against the destructive Electromagnetic/WiFi frequencies and radiation ranging from naturally occurring radon to nuclear? And how is it that Shungite was virtually unknown in the United States until 2014 yet a vast amount of the rest of the world knew about the Magical Black Stone that fell to Earth in Russia. And is it true Shungite can save the bees and all other insects to prevent the "Sixth Extinction Event".

To all those questions the answer is yes. This book will explain why. But to understand what Shungite Reality is all about, you need to acknowledge this: there may exist scientific information that has been kept secret.

Just because something is kept secret from some people does not mean it is a secret to other people. We acknowledge that we are using some tools unaccepted by Western Science. However, the majority of the world, from indigenous people to world religions, would not have a problem with seemingly imaginary energy being harnessed into energy devices. That is what the problem is. For a government that understands that we live in an energy universe and energy manipulation can create astounding weapons, secrecy becomes necessary for self-defense.

We are not going to focus on the why and who is keeping the secrets. If you want a much fuller picture for those answers, please see my book Cosmic Reality, which is available through Amazon or as a free PDF on our website CosmicReality.net.

What we are going to present in this book, is an introduction to Shungite and to the science that explains why its magical properties exist and how we were able to develop products that could change lives.

So far down the Rabbit Hole we found the back door.

The "Rabbit Hole" is defined as:

> To enter into a situation or begin a process or journey that is particularly strange, problematic, difficult, complex, or chaotic, especially one that becomes increasingly so as it develops or unfolds. (An allusion to Alice's Adventures in Wonderland by Lewis Carroll.)

Taking the path of "The Shungite Experience" is absolutely as defined above. It started with a very difficult and complex problem, namely the dangers posed by electric and electronic systems and devices to everything alive.

The particularly strange aspect to this voyage is a carbon-based mineral that came from outside Earth and crashed into what is now called Karelia, Russia 2.5 billion years ago. What remained were 1,000 square kilometers, as deep as 400 feet, of what has come to be called "Shungite".

And the journey: the EMF problem, as formidable as it was, could be solved by using Shungite. The goal - prove it.

In the Spring of 2014, I was a researcher, writer, internet radio host and someone forced into "retirement" by a business closing and my age of 65. I was researching on the Internet when a Facebook Group started to ding-ding-ding indicating some subject was trending.

Much to my surprise, the group was discussing the dangers of EM/WiFi signals. This was a subject I was very familiar with. My brother had died of a tumor in his brain directly tied to WiFi frequencies.

==I believe in the Universe of Spiritual Intervention (USI). By that I mean I am guided to accomplish some mission my soul agreed to do before I was ever born.== I also believe intervention is accomplished by spiritual beings. When I saw the Facebook posts, I said to these invisible guides, "Please, give me something to give them." I went back to researching and in less than ½ an hour later I saw the phrase, "the Russian military is using Shungite to shield electronic equipment." I went back to the Facebook group and told them to look into Shungite.

Within a week my friend Rev. Lee Brown came to visit me. At the time I had no WiFi capability in this house and she needed WiFi for her job as a telephone psychic advisor. Lee set up the WiFi terminal, turned it on, and I immediately said, "Whoa I cannot take that energy."

Lee looked at her hand and the ring she was wearing, took it off her finger and walked over to the WiFi terminal. She put the ring over the antenna and the energy in the room immediately shifted. I had never experienced such a drastic change from very yucky feeling energy into delightful feeling energy. "What did you do?"

Lee told me what she did was put the ring holding Shungite onto the antenna. She had no idea why she did it. But I know it was just The Universe of Spiritual Intervention at work. Lee has been a mineral collector and dealer for decades. She had only just heard of Shungite and ordered some. The package got to her the day before she flew down to see me.

This was in March 2014, and four years later we had proved Shungite could attenuate EM frequencies to be biocompatible with all life - problem solved. Well, not exactly. Remember, we were in the Rabbit Hole.

We had also confirmed that Shungite and Shungite Devices can purify water, air, and soil of toxins; and that Shungite will balance biological energy fields promoting physical and mental health. In actuality, we were just proving statements made by others, all over the world, for centuries regarding water purity and the healing properties of Shungite.

But we had found ourselves in a peculiarly strange place between contemporary science and a different science we were exploring that breached the divide between "metaphysics" and "quantum physics". We found ourselves studying energy, and so this alternative science was named "Enerology" - the study of energy.

ENEROLOGY

Enerology is simply the study of energy. It is based upon the concept that we live in an energy universe and the material 3D world, as depicted by contemporary science, is energy vibrating at the same basic rate resulting in the "frozen energy" of the material universe.

Quantum Physics evolved out of advanced technology allowing observations of the smallest known objects in the material 3D world. Those atoms, protons, electrons, and neutrons were not operating in ways conforming to Newtonian Physics. The more the quantum world was studied the more a new concept of reality evolved. This concept shook the scientific community: you simply cannot have matter without an energy blueprint and that energy blueprint is creative thinking.

Energy blueprints in the material universe are "Thought-Forms" manifested during conscious thinking. This concept of thought dictating the construct of any given reality is at the very core of Quantum Physics. It is also why Quantum Physics has not been universally embraced by many scientific disciplines and scientists. Quantum physicists concluded very early in their studies and experiments conducted at the atomic and subatomic levels, that whatever the researcher thought would happen was exactly what did happen. And they proved it in many ways and in many experiments. At the very smallest observable level of our 3D reality thought controls what happens.

Max Planck, the originator of Quantum theory, put it this way, "I regard consciousness as fundamental. I regard matter as derivative from consciousness. We cannot get behind consciousness. Everything that we talk about, everything that we regard as existing, postulates consciousness."

So, ok...but where is all this energy coming from that can meld itself into material 3D manifestation following an energetic blueprint of a thought? Well, this is where Shungite comes into the discussion. In studying the properties of Shungite, we began witnessing what happens when a finite object (Shungite) can access infinite power within the Quantum Field.

THE QUANTUM FIELD

The Quantum Field as defined within Enerology is the place where "Proto-Energy" resides. Proto-energy can be seen as waves or particles of pure energy that are the building blocks of all 3D manifestations. All that ever was, is or will be begins as proto-energy in the Quantum Field. The key to manifestation is to access the Quantum Field and its proto-energy. The key to Shungite's magic is, it does access the Quantum Field.

WHAT IS SHUNGITE?

Shungite is a carbon-based mineral that came from outside Earth and crashed into what is now called Karelia, Russia 2.5 billion years ago. What remained was 1,000 square kilometers as deep as 400 feet of what has come to be called "Shungite".

In the simplest terms, Shungite is like a frozen stew. Somewhere in the cosmic landscape between the stars a bunch of atoms came together to make a bunch of carbon molecules, the main ingredient in Shungite. Wherever the cosmic birth location existed, it was full of the basic building blocks of matter - especially the carbon atoms. In fact Shungite has been attributed as having trace amounts of virtually the entire periodic table of possible chemical elements throughout the impact zone.

So this frozen cosmic creation came in as a meteorite and crashed into the area where Russia meets Finland. Today Karelia, called by National Geographic, "Land of a Thousand Lakes" includes the two largest lakes in Europe, and water systems running through the meteorite deposit - "The Shungite Field" - displayed the first surprising property of Shungite. All the water systems maintain a virtually pristine state of purity. The Shungite was somehow purifying water.

Note: some contend Shungite is not a meteorite but a result of the earliest vestiges of life decaying and creating Shungite. I disagree with this explanation of its origins for many reasons.

WHERE IS SHUNGITE FOUND?

There is only one "Shungite" source in the world. It is the Shungite deposits in the western Republic of Karelia. While there are other similar "stew" deposits throughout the world, Karelia is the only place to find Shungite, which is named after a local town called Shunga.

I cannot stress enough that you must make sure you have genuine Shungite. Since the world began understanding the magic of Shungite and interest spread, there is fake Shungite being sold in great quantities. When I was first introduced to Shungite in 2014, the Russians were claiming it would one day be worth more than gold. I am inclined to think they are right. The prices have radically continued to climb and there are suggestions it will become much more difficult to obtain, as its reputation spreads even further into mankind's reality. (But don't worry - we will never run out.)

So how did Shungite begin to get popular? It began with the 1996 Nobel Prize in Chemistry awarded to Americans Robert F. Curl, Jr. and Richard E. Smalley with British Sir Harold W. Kroto. They had created in a laboratory a newly identified molecule designated as a "Fullerene".

FULLERENE - C60 MOLECULE

The actual research project was conducted in 1985 and was a lab experiment to see what kinds of molecules could theoretically be created in interstellar space. Remember, a molecule is made up of atoms. Depending upon the pattern the atoms follow, various "forms" are designated. Until the 1985 experiment, there were six identified forms of the carbon molecule or six patterns for atomic arrangements. This newly discovered C60 arrangement was completely unique, as the pattern resulted in the atoms forming a shell. Technically, there was an inside and an outside to the "fullerene molecules" - the name given to the new atomic pattern.

While the atoms followed the same pattern, there were different numbers of carbon atoms associated with different types of fullerenes and there was one molecule that stood out as being special. It was comprised of 60 atoms and was uniquely stable. The shell created by these atoms formed a perfect geometric shape identical to the American soccer ball. This is the C60 Fullerene everyone is talking about.

In addition to being a soccer ball design, it was also identical to what you would get if you took two geodesic domes and attached them together at the base. The geodesic dome had been popularized by the American architect R. Buckminster Fuller as the most stable architectural shape. It was only fitting this new form of molecular structure, with the most stable molecule yet identified - the C60 - should be named the buckminsterfullerene family of carbon molecules. The C60 itself has been nicknamed the "Bucky Ball".

An essentially new branch of chemistry arose focusing on the potential applications of the fullerenes. In 2014, if you Google searched "fullerene", there were some 478,000 results. By November 2018, the search came back with 3,520,000 results with the vast majority being scientific papers. But the original molecules were created and isolated in a lab. Were there any naturally occurring fullerene molecules? You guessed it - yes there are and they are found in Shungite. Thus, the mark of the discovery of the C60 molecule opened the doorway leading to Shungite.

SHUNGITE'S C60

It is referred to as an "accidental discovery", but we know there are really no accidents and coincidence is another word for thought in action. The lab-created C60 had gained in popularity and a student at Arizona State, USA - Dr. Wang Su - had recorded an electron micrograph image of synthetic C60. A Russian scientist, Dr. Semeon J. Tsirpursky saw the image and realized it was identical to carbon atom images found in Shungite. Dr. Tsirpursky had been part of a Soviet study on Shungite before going to the US.

Shungite was analyzed by a mass spectrometer that found it contained both the C60 and the C70 fullerenes. C70 has 70 atoms and the shell looks more like an American football. These fullerene molecules are contained within the carbon content of Shungite and that varies depending upon where the sample came from within the Shungite field.

TYPES OF SHUNGITE

Raw Shungite

While not specifically stated, I suspect the Shungite being examined has up to 98% carbon content and is called both Elite and Noble Shungite. The best I can figure out is that when "Elite" is used the Shungite has a brownish color whereas "Noble" is on the dark black side and may be another name for "Petrovsky" Shungite. By any name it is the same basic mineral makeup and we will only refer to it as Elite Shungite. Elite is mined by hand because it is found as veins within the Shungite field and is relatively fragile. It is very costly to mine and therefore the first to be targeted by fraudulent people. I have compared Elite to two common coal types, Anthracite and Bituminous. I could not find anything visual to distinguish the Elite from the coal.

Elite Shungite

We do not sell this "Grade A Elite Shungite" in any form and all the following data applies to the "regular" or "Raw" Shungite. Essentially, the darker black the raw stone the more carbon it contains, and more carbon indicates more C60 Fullerenes.

Some so-called Shungite Beads and different objects ranging from geometric shapes to animal carvings are erroneously called Shungite but can come from either the Ukraine or Kazakhstan and there may be other sources. Recently the Chinese have taken compressed coal to make figurines, pendants, and other items and they are passing it off as Shungite. The difference can be seen by looking for lines of gold or silver, which is pyrite, only found in Shungite.

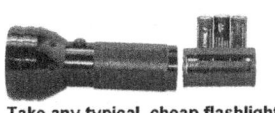

SHUNGITE TEST

1. Take any typical, cheap flashlight and turn it on.
2. Unscrew the cap which has a spring in it.
3. DO NOT remove the battery compartment.

4. Place the nugget or figurine so it touches the center metal piece in the battery holder while the other end touches the spring in the cap.

There is a test for Shungite authenticity whereby electric conductivity is measured. There are many versions of this test. The easiest way is to take a typical flashlight, turn it on, unscrew the back cap (causing the light to go out), put the Shungite nugget on the middle top of the battery carrier and touch the spring beneath the on/off button of the flashlight. If it is real Shungite the light will come back on. See our YouTube Channel "Shungite Reality" for a video demonstration.

SHUNGITE "NUGGETS"

In April of 2014, three United States sources for Shungite were identified. The first source was an eBay vendor who had rings and pendants made with Shungite. The other two sources (also eBay vendors) had bags of nuggets to be used to purify water. Both nugget vendors provided a similar supply of nuggets that ranged mostly in size from 1/8-1/4 inches with a few as large as 1 inch.

The search for more sources of Shungite led to eBay, European vendors, and websites from Russian sources. International sales took longer to ship and, honestly, I was confused as to who was who and who had what. I began a buying spree to answer those questions.

There were supposedly two deposits in Karelia - Maksovskaya and Zazhoginsky. The Zazhoginsky mines were recommended as the only place to get nuggets. Bulldozers simply scrape across the tops of the deposits and dump their loads, which are then sorted by nugget size after larger rocks are broken up.

So the key was getting Shungite from the Zazhoginsky mines. But what size? It turns out that different vendors had various sizes of the nuggets and there were differences in the "quality" of the selection. One European vendor with great prices actually had machined pieces, broken during the manufacture of Shungite, into a variety of forms from figurines to building slabs. The typical supply was of nuggets used to purify water.

WATER PURIFICATION

It was the water purification capabilities of Shungite that had the world's attention. Someone recently asked me to provide "empirical evidence that Shungite purifies water". I laughed. This is a question I will not answer, as it is considered a known fact. I doubt a question about empirical evidence that carbon purifies water would have been asked, as it is used in most water filters.

To get to the actual scientific research, you might want to learn how to read Russian and know enough to make out what other scientific papers (the vast majority translated from Russian) are saying. The accepted conclusion is that

Shungite cleans water of various chlorine compounds, nitrates, copper, magnesium, iron, it cleans up visually dirty water, eliminates sour taste, removes heavy metals, toxic bacteria, and other toxins.

Commercial use of Shungite filters started back in the 1990's and have replaced carbon filters all over the world. Shungite is currently being used to clean up water associated with radiation pollution from the Fukushima nuclear plant accident in March 2011.

Shungite Energized Water Vs Shungite Water

Directions for making "Shungite Water" differ. In basic terms, a handful of nuggets in a typical water pitcher should sit for three days and then it is ok to go, but do not drink too much because water sitting in a pile of Shungite is purified, but the PH is also changed to acidic levels, which can be very damaging to health.

We believe you only need three nuggets - large enough to handle easily - in any size water container. We talk about "Shungite Energized Water", explained later. There is no PH change and there is no health risk to drinking as much as you can safely consume.

HEALTH BENEFITS

As long as you are not concentrating the effects of Shungite in water, like taking it from the lakes that are absolutely pure, there have been reports of impressive healings associated with Shungite Water for centuries before Russian Tsar Peter the Great became aware of its reputation for healing. The Tsar's personal physicians were directed to determine the truth about claims that Shungite could heal. Robert Erskine and Laurence Blumentrost confirmed Shungite Water was useful for the treatment of several diseases. That conclusion resulted in the establishment of the resort "Marcial Waters" by decree of the Tsar on March 20,1719. The Tsar and his family used it as a resort and it also had facilities for Russian soldiers to heal their wounds. The Tsar's military forces were also outfitted with Shungite nuggets to purify their water.

The stories and studies are well documented concerning Shungite's health benefits. In 1993, the children's sanatorium "The Seagull" in Karelia using Shungite for cooking, inhalations, and baths reported a one hundred percent cure rate for asthma in children who inhaled high concentrations of water, improvement in food allergies, gastritis and enterocolitis, and Shungite filtered water resulted in relief from infectious diseases and hepatitis. Shungite paneled rooms built in Russian military hospitals are shortening recovery time for heart patients and others.

As inspiring as all this is, it reminded me of the "Fountain of Youth". In 1513 Spanish explorer Juan Ponce de Leon got off his boat and stepped onto the Florida peninsula near today's St Augustine. Legend has it he was searching for the "Fountain of Youth". Where that story comes from went something like this:

The sailors were taking water from the surface lakes, streams and swamps. The Native Americans took pity on the strangers and had a conversation that went like this.

"Hey, Dude, why are you drinking that terrible water? Just dig a hole and you will find water that is like a fountain of youth."

The natives showed them how to dig the hole and there it was, 2-6 feet below the surface. For sailors coming from Europe (where water could be very scarce, dirty and awful tasting) on a boat where any water they had was in barrels that had probably never been cleaned, the limestone rock below their feet was a fountain; an aquifer, or cave like sections in the limestone which stored water. Because of the limestone, the water takes on a high alkaline PH - known to be the most healing water. After drinking this water, the sailors felt and looked years younger.

Maybe that was the key to Shungite. It purified water, and pure water is critical to good health. I was not impressed. In addition, I was on a mission. The Russian Military were using Shungite as shielding for their electronic equipment. It was supposedly shielding against an Electro-Magnetic Pulse (EMP) created during a nuclear explosion, which would destroy any electronic circuits it encountered. Terrorists had supposedly made a small EMP weapon that could destroy civilian electronic systems and bring chaos with it.

I had already witnessed the effect Shungite had on electrical/electronic signals. Something magical happened and it was NOT blocking or shielding. Shungite was able to "attenuate" or change those signals from being damaging to being biocompatible with life and non-harmful. But I suspected this was not known by establishment science.

ENVIRONMENTAL PROTECTION

In addition to Shungite water filters coming into use during

90's, a company in St. Petersburg called Alfa-Paul mass-producing and selling Shungite building ...cts such as plaster that was resistant to fire and ...... and appeared to somehow cut down on mold growth in buildings. Shungite materials were also being sold as protection against electromagnetic radiation, radon (a natural health hazard in geoactive zones below the surface and in communities), static electricity, and X-rays. Shungite screened rooms were being advertised as "healing rooms".

THE PATH BEGINS

In all honesty, I am not sure my Shungite Experience would have gone beyond an initial look at this supposed "magical mineral" being advertised as "The Medicine of the 21st Century". But the Universe of Spiritual Intervention had another view of what my mission was and how my entire life had been designed to make me uniquely able to experience the true infinite possibilities Shungite offered.

My experience in a decade of buying, selling, collecting, and researching minerals gave me the knowledge to understand basic mineral science and the ins-and-outs of buying and selling Shungite. My two decades working at a small manufacturing company gave me the knowledge of production requirements that would make me comfortable building a company designed to develop and market innovative Shungite products. And my tour with the US Army as an Electronic Warfare Officer taught me the basics of electric/electronic systems and concepts and unveiled the true dangers of invisible signals with the power to kill.

But the biggest gift I had been given was to be extremely sensitive to energies of all types, including those of electromagnetic radiation, particularly WiFi frequencies. And just to clear the path, in 2013 the manufacturing company I was working at as the office/shipping manager closed. At the age of 65 I was without a job, so there was nothing to keep me from jumping down the rabbit hole. I had plenty of time to unravel the mysteries of Shungite.

When Lee Brown put the ring over the antenna of the WiFi device, resulting in the impressive energy shift, my life changed. I was stunned momentarily before getting up and doing an Internet search for "Shungite". Shortly after that I put one of Lee's Shungite pendants on my 14-year-old dog Josie's collar. By then I had read about the healing properties of Shungite and Josie was about 48 hours from passing over. The next day she was so much better I actually forgot to give her medicine to her. Josie lasted another six months in relatively good health.

Gaia's Gift

By the time Josie passed I was completely immersed in the mission "to get Shungite to the masses". Two months after being introduced to Shungite I was selling bags of the nuggets, and pendants created by wire-wrapping nuggets. Within 45 minutes of making the internet store live, the first sale came in. In the last five years the store has doubled its sales every year. It now has dozens of products and is called "Gaia's Gift".

Someone posted a comment that the use of the name Gaia's Gift for an internet store was blasphemy. They totally did not get me. I consider Shungite a gift of Nature, however it got here. I believe Gaia is the Creator Consciousness of this biosphere we call Earth. I see

Shungite as a way to level the playing field to stop the ongoing slaughter of all things natural by the technological society we have created. This is a war I have been engaged in since the 1970's.

ELECTRONIC WARFARE

I was accepted as a Direct Commissioned Officer in the US Army. I ended up working for the Army Security Agency and soon became the acknowledged expert on Soviet Electronic Warfare capabilities. I got a call from a superior officer asking me to answer a question he had just received from the US State Department. "Is there any Soviet weapon that can cause cancer?" The employees at the American Embassy in Moscow were coming down with various cancers in abnormally high numbers.

As I considered the question, I began thinking about a capability Americans had to gather intelligence. They had found that by saturating a room with microwave radiation from an emitter source with a receiver nearby, anything vocally said in the room would alter the microwave radiation. That alteration in the signal could be deciphered to hear all that was spoken, in the same way that radio signals carry information. "Have NSA scan the building for microwave radiation," was my answer.

Shame it turned out to be true. Microwave radiation could provide intelligence but it would also kill. The Soviets were not out to cause cancer - it was an intelligence-gathering operation. I do not think the telecommunications industries intended to kill off the insect population and be the #1 cause of health problems in humans, animals and plants. They were just trying to make money developing a WiFi system. Shame it kills, like it did when used in Moscow.

In the period before the internet, learning more and trying to convince people of the dangers of first the electric systems and then the WiFi threat was absolutely impossible. Even my brother Phil, who was working with radars and the new analog cell phones, would not listen to my warnings. It took 20 years, but he died of a brain cancer that has now been directly linked to electromagnetic signals coming from radars and cell phones. He was only 55 years old. His death propelled me into more research and a decade of trying again to communicate the dangers and to use the internet as a means of communication, but still, no one was listening.

And then one day in 2014, FaceBook started dinging; Shungite was brought to me and the game was on and I was now in a very unique position. The Universe of Spiritual Intervention had worked its magic and I was an internet radio host. I had a platform that reached thousands worldwide. In the months between meeting Shungite and activating Gaia's Gift store, I was on a dozen shows talking about Shungite and getting other hosts and listeners excited about what we were discovering.

One of those listeners was Walt Silva whom I was soon calling "The Master Magician". My introduction to Walt came in September 2014. I had asked the World of Spirit, "Please find me someone who can take what I have in my head and make it real."

The magic behind what Walt brought to the table will be discussed later. It is heavy on the science side. For now we are going to just focus on what Walt made real as Shungite products and the explanation of how they work. But we do have to talk about the basic science behind the magic. Oh, by the way, "magic" is just the manipulation of energy and Shungite is one heck of a teacher and Walt is one heck of a magician.

SHUNGITE SCIENCE - SIMPLIFIED

The stew of Raw Shungite has 35-65% carbon. Within that carbon are found C60 molecules. 12 pentagons and 20 hexagons are formed by the 60 carbon atoms into a sphere looking exactly like an American soccer ball. These "Bucky Balls" are large, extremely stable molecules, rotating at an estimated 20 billion times a second.

I honestly have not found if this makes C60 the fastest rotating molecule or not, but it would not be a surprise. It is the closest you can probably get to a perfect sphere, which must mean something. But it is the angles and distances between the atoms that cause the rotation. The distances are all the same and the angles are all the same. At the point where lines and angles converge is a carbon atom.

In the science of Enerology, within the Physical Universe energy follows geometry. At each of the carbon atoms, the energy flowing through the C60 molecule collides creating what is called a zero point, null point or an atomic vacuum. As the Universe abhors a vacuum, a door is opened into the Quantum Field. The Quantum Field is the source of proto-energy - the stuff that everything existing, has existed or presumably will exist is made of.

With 60 atoms sitting in an atomic vacuum environment, the Quantum Field door is opened and then shut causing proto-energy to pulse into the C60 structure, spinning the molecule at 20 billion times a second. That spinning causes an energy field of extreme stability and force to exist. It is this spinning energy field that is the magic behind Shungite.

From the very beginning I knew there were not many C60 fullerenes in the Shungite carbon and, as I said, it only took one of those little dynamos to do everything we were seeing it do. The C60 is a finite object linked to the infinite power of the Quantum Field. To understand what it does, we will now turn our attention to various products developed to do the many things Shungite can do.

SHUNGITE NUGGETS - WATER

It is critical to understand that we had no access to any meter except our own bodies to determine whether an EM/WiFi signal is good or bad. The same can be said about the nuggets and water. Yes, there are thousands of scientific studies on Shungite and water purification. But that was based on a handful of nuggets. We were stating it only took three nuggets to cause the water to become pure. WHAT???

You can get the Shungite nuggets from any reputable source. Just make sure it is from the Zazhoginsky deposit. Take three nuggets of any size and use them to create a "coherent field", meaning the field of each nugget unites with the other two energy fields to produce a whole new field of greater "cohesion" or bond. Just think - three nuggets create a very energetic field capable of disintegrating toxic molecules.

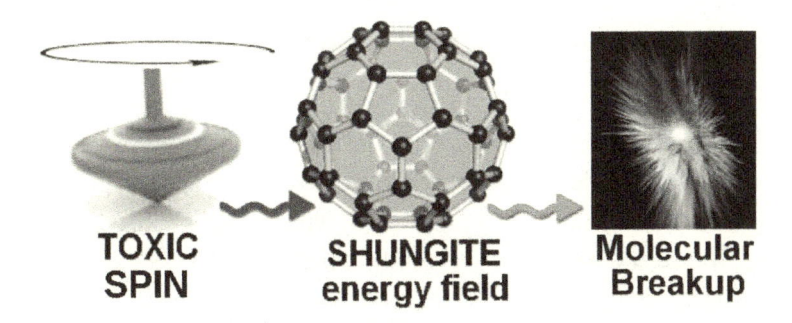

TOXIC SPIN → **SHUNGITE energy field** → **Molecular Breakup**

In water, this coherent Shungite field is spinning and stable and so powerful that the fields of energy associated with toxic molecules cannot survive. A molecule of chlorine is toxic because its rotation is counter to that of a living cell. The simplest way of envisioning this is to think of the toxic molecule spinning counterclockwise while a biological cell is rotating clockwise. When the toxic molecule hits the clockwise spinning Shungite field, it is like two tops coming together, with each spinning in an opposite direction. Whichever top is spinning faster has more power behind it and the other top loses its spin momentum.

But a molecule is not a top and when the molecular toxic spin is stopped in a field of Shungite, the molecule loses its molecular cohesion and the atoms break away. The toxic molecule has simply disappeared.

This was proven by two separate studies on how quickly a Shungite water purifier, with a canister full of Shungite instead of carbon, becomes overcome with absorbed pollutants. As carbon sucks up toxins and then has to be replaced, the researchers were looking for the point at which Shungite should be replaced. After all, everyone knew the water was being purified by Shungite and they assumed it was due to the absorption of toxins. Both studies (which confused researchers) concluded there was no absorption. The toxins were simply not there.

Nuggets and Your Water System

It took a while before I focused on the water. By the time I did, my studies of EM/WiFi and Shungite had led to a deeper understanding of Enerology regarding what Shungite was doing and how it was doing it. Three nuggets made a coherent energy field pulsing with quantum proto-energy. This field is so powerful, it can work on water even when it is not in the water.

Two vases with exactly the same flowers sat 5 feet away from each other on a kitchen counter where the light was the same for each vase. After three days, one vase had clear water and the flowers were twice as big as those of its twin. The water in the second vase was cloudy. The only difference was that a bowl of about 10 Shungite nuggets was 4 inches away from the vase that was demonstrating health in both the water and the flowers themselves.

I went out to my main water pipe, which was above ground and easily accessible. I took three nuggets in my palm and wrapped my hand around the cold water pipe, holding the nuggets up against the pipe. I was focusing on the water pipe in the direction of the house. I assumed the field would energize the water beyond the nuggets, like if you added something to a river - it would flow downstream.

Instantaneously I detected a change in the field. Indeed, the Shungite field had energized the water and it was actually spinning! You see, water in a pipe will stop spinning molecularly if it goes 100 feet down a pipe or if the pipe makes a 90-degree turn. The water in my pipe had been essentially "dead" until the nuggets supercharged the system.

Remember, I was "intuitively" or "psychically" observing the water at the molecular level. You could think it was pure imagination and I would not argue that, but my "imaginings" resulted in a variety of Shungite products that have eventually been tested using more accepted empirical methods and by many thousands of customers.

So there I was, sitting on the ground with Shungite nuggets in my hand which was wrapped around a water pipe watching the water going to the house change. I suddenly realized that something else was happening. The water coming from the meter, before it had reached the Shungite nuggets, was also beginning to spin. I sat there stupefied, etherically watching the 200-foot pipe where the dead water was now spinning. It was like a wave of energy traveling up the pipe, all the way to the street where the meter and main valve are located.

My next question was, "Why?" As the most important part of learning is to ask the right question, the answer was swift. "Resonance" came into my head and it all made perfect sense.

RESONANCE

The phenomenon of resonance is a critical law in the Energy Universe. In Physics it is defined one way as the "synchronous vibration of a neighboring object". Here are some examples of resonance at work.

If you open up the top of a standard upright piano to display the strings, resonance in action can be observed. If the Middle C note is played, all the other C notes begin to visibly vibrate, although softly and the sound is not detectable by the human ear. The C strings are synchronously vibrating together.

Human energy fields vibrate in unison with the Schumann Resonance Earth frequency, often refereed to as the "heart beat of Earth". This was proven when Cosmonauts on long duration space flights came back mentally unbalanced. To counteract the effect, Schumann Resonators are now on board every manned spacecraft. The artificial energy field of Earth keeps the human brain synced with or resonating in unison with the Schumann frequency to maintain a healthy brain.

But one of the most profound demonstrations of resonance is the one I saw as I held three Shungite nuggets on a water pipe. Water molecules within the Shungite field began spinning and that spin created a frequency field causing neighboring molecules to begin synchronous vibrations resulting in a spinning motion. And like a wave, every layer of water molecules began spinning. The water had been energized and was "alive".

The difference in the water is stunning. The water feels softer or silky, which I believe is due to the spinning water breaking the surface tension. It tastes better, which is probably due to the elimination of toxins. But it also appears that the water itself is connecting to the Quantum Field as long as any part of the water is in a Shungite Field. It took more than four years for me to understand this concept that the water itself was making the quantum connection.

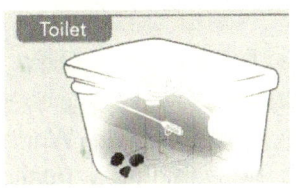

My toilet bowl - even with Shungite on the water system - needed cleaning every 4-5 days. When I opened the toilet tank, there was a really yucky brown slime/algae growing on the edges of the tank under and above the water line. That was when I realized that the toilet valve that shuts off when the tank is full of water was closing off the water in the tank from the Shungite Field connection.

The water in the tank was not energized. So I put three medium-sized nuggets in the tank (off to the side so they would not be drawn into the drain). Within a week the slime was breaking up and now cleaning the bowl is seldom necessary.

This concept that water will lose its spin is the reason we recommend three nuggets in any pet bowl, drinking glass, pitcher or even plastic bottles. There are some warning that plastic bottles will leach toxins into Shungite water but that does not make any sense. If toxins leach into the water, the Shungite will destroy them.

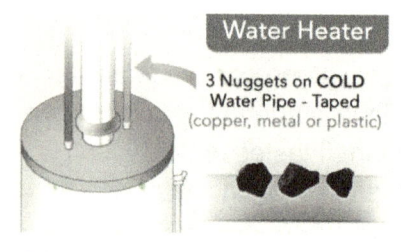

So, a valve can be a problem. The water heater also has a shut off valve when its tank is filled. Does that mean the hot water system is not being Shungite energized? Not necessarily. If you have put the three nuggets on the cold water intake to the water heater that we have been recommending, the cold and hot pipes are close enough together that the Shungite Field from the three nuggets will also energize the hot water pipe.

==According to a fully certified Quantum Physicist, the Shungite Field has been measured to radiate out many feet depending upon the quality of the Shungite.== When I asked him how it was measured, he went into a detailed explanation and I had no idea what he was talking about. It was an odd telephone conversation that I do not want to explain. Just note I did not feel comfortable pursuing a lesson in quantum measurements, but was grateful he had confirmed the large radius of a Shungite Field. He also confirmed the basics of the science we were observing.

So for now, just remember to put three nuggets on the cold water pipe going into your water heater using duct or other durable tape . Make sure it is close enough to the hot water pipe that both will become energized, and by close enough I mean the hot water pipe at the heater, which is normally a few inches away from the cold water pipe. If you tape the nuggets to the hot water pipe the tape will deteriorate and need replacing.

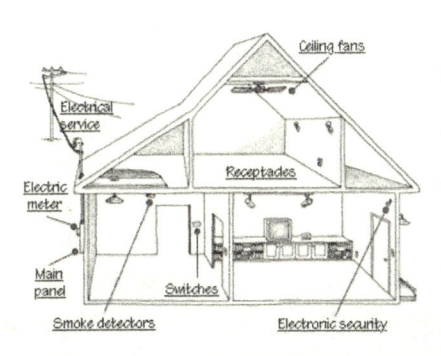

NUGGETS AND YOUR ELECTRIC SYSTEM

What is an electric system? Well, it is wires attached to your meter box. Then that meter box is attached by wires to the Power Company's electrical system. Electricity in your house flowing along the wires inside the house puts out an electromagnetic field that is dangerous. We say it is not "biocompatable".

We are energy bodies vibrating at a rate that is the same throughout 3D reality. Because we are all vibrating in unison to the same range of frequencies, we look solid to each other. The electric and magnetic fields of your body can be measured and used to diagnose the health of your body.

This concept of electromagnetic energy coming from the human body has been used by metaphysicians for thousands of years, has been talked about and demonstrated, and is linked to the chakra system that most of us have heard about. The bioelectromagnetic field and the 3D physical cells of all biological life on the planet all rotate in the same direction.

Unfortunately the electric field given off by your electric system in your house radiates 4 to 6 feet in all directions

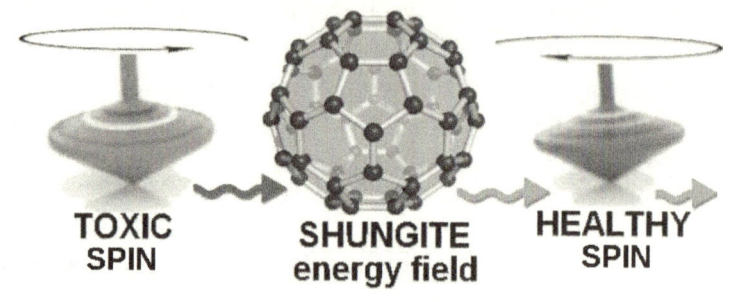

TOXIC SPIN   **SHUNGITE energy field**   **HEALTHY SPIN**

and is rotating in the opposite direction to what is biocompatible. The electric field is more powerful than the rotation of individual cells and those cells begin to deteriorate. It's like two tops coming together, just like when we are dealing with toxicity in water, but this is an electromagnetic energy field that can also be attenuated, which means it can be changed to be biocompatible.

The electromagnetic signals powering your lights and appliances are not molecules that break up in a Shungite field, as discussed above in water purification. The rotation of the EM signal can be easily changed so both the signal and the cells are rotating in the same direction, without any deterioration in the quality or power of the EM signal, nor are the cells harmed. All that is required is Shungite.

I put a nugget of Shungite on the cable box and I was weighing it as I did it. In two groups we could feel the energy change as we put more Shungite on the cable box until there were 15 grams of Shungite on the box. At 15 grams we had the maximum change in the energy. I initially put together what we called the Bucky Bag, which contained 22 grams of smaller nuggets as we were using the bigger nuggets for water purification. With the Bucky Bag on any device that is always on, the electric field from the wires of a home should be attenuated and be biocompatable.

Well, this is what we initially thought. We were to discover that any time an electrical device with its own (secondary) motor was turned on, the energy field would be in a toxic rotation. The bottom line was that electric devices, from a hairdryer to the refrigerator, needed their own Shungite field.

SHUNGITE POWDER

When I say "we", it is a reference to Walt Silva and myself. Now what is so awesome about our relationship is that I am energy sensitive. I can tell him what I'm feeling, sensing, seeing, whatever it is that allows me to understand what's happening energetically, and then Walt takes that information and makes it real. The first thing he does is figure out a way to be able to test my observations and then he figures out what to do with this information. The next thing I know we have a new product.

I had detected that a large piece of Shungite was not as energetic as a small one. Walt took this concept of "less Shungite is more energy" and began to make Shungite powder.

When I explained that we needed something other than Shungite nuggets to affect secondary electric systems,

Walt suggested using Shungite powder. It took a while to figure it out, but we finally developed Shungite stickers. By using printed labels we could put the Shungite powder on the sticky part on the back of the label. Now, instead of having nuggets all over the place, you could put Shungite stickers on secondary systems, from a hairdryer to a refrigerator. The effect is that the energy field of the secondary motors is attenuated.

This also allowed us to put Shungite stickers on phones. It was a better option to use stickers with Shungite powder than to use a slab of Shungite stuck to your phone (that fell off one woman's phone and she thought it was a Junior Mint candy LOL.) It soon became apparent that a phone with a Shungite sticker on it did not get hot, or at least not as hot as a cell phone without the sticker, and energy-sensitive people were feeling a change for the better from the effect it had on the cell phone radiation. This was in late 2014.

I felt that the Shungite sticker on the cell phone was making a positive impact on the signal. However, something negative was still in that field. I had no clue what it was, but I was still not happy with what Shungite was doing with WiFi. I had no problems with electric systems but when it came to WiFi systems, as in the cell phone, Shungite was missing something. And then The Universe of Spiritual Intervention came into play again.

I was on Skype with a friend who had a pendant. We were on video and I suddenly noticed the pendant looked weird. I looked at it a little bit more and then realized I was seeing copper wire where I should have seen silver. Now this was a friend of mine who I had given one of my first Shungite wraps to. Those very first wraps were made with copper wires with a silver covering. For some reason, the silver was no longer covering the copper wire. When I asked her about it she said, "I have been meaning to tell you that, and I don't know why the silver has disappeared off the entire wire. It's not like it's been rubbed off."

So I call up Walt Silva and I tell him what happened. He says. "Oh well, silver will migrate."

"What do you mean by migrate?" I asked.

"That's why they like to use gold when soldering electronic devices. When silver is in the solder, the silver will often leave the solder and when you open up the electronic device to fix it, the silver is not in the solder. This does not happen with gold."

"So you mean the silver on the copper wire has migrated off the wire and into the Shungite?"

"Well, I don't know," and Walt Silva simply does not like not knowing.

Right after I told him about the migrating silver, Walt took a batch of colloidal silver and dropped a bunch of Shungite nuggets in it. Some 24 hours later, the particles of silver in the solution were not there. It looked like clear water. Walt took out the nuggets, studied them, then scratched them to see if the silver would come off. It was not simply attached to the outside as he could not scratch anything like silver off the nuggets. He concluded that the Shungite had absorbed the silver, or to put it another way, the Shungite had been saturated with nanoparticles of silver.

So then Walt took raw Shungite powder, put it in a new batch of colloidal silver, and as with the nuggets, the nanoparticles of silver migrated into the powder. Shungite

S4 Powder had been born. And what does the S4 stand for? "S̲ilver S̲aturated S̲hungite by Walt S̲ilva.

SHUNGITE S4 POWDER

In my interpretation of Shungite Reality, the connection between the Shungite and the quantum field is like a door that opens and closes. It creates a pulsing effect. The door opens and the energy of the quantum field pours through into the 3D. Then the door shuts, stopping the flow of energy. While you only need a blast of quantum energy to change or attenuate the field given off by an electric wire and some electronic devices, when you are dealing with a WiFi signal, pulsing will not work to make it biocompatible.

"Electrical" - meaning something that does something like a refrigerator - or "electronic" - meaning it communicates, similar to a television; both have the signals a Shungite field can reverse in rotation virtually instantaneously. But when there is a WiFi signal associated with an electronic device, we needed more than just the pulse. With the Shungite S4 powder, the silver seemed to keep the door between the 3D and the quantum field always open. Instead of there being a pulse from the open and closing of the door, there is a continuous blast of quantum field energy. This new and enhanced energy field of silver and Shungite was now strong enough to attenuate the WiFi signal. The difference was stunning.

With the S4 powder to play with, Walt and I began experimenting with various types of blank labels, how to print the labels, how to get the powder on the back of the labels, how to protect the powder, and of course the most important part of the process, the powder itself. We ended up with the Bucky Bandaid, the S4 Shungite Sticker, and the Smart Sticker.

Acceptable
Heimendinger
003-001-81
tudy of energ

We actually had the Bucky Bandaid already. We had been producing it, selling it, and people were putting it on electric systems and devices. The reports back were that they were working.

The S4 stickers were initially just for cell phones, but as customers reported back and with our own experience and understanding of Shungite, we recommend the S4 stickers for any WiFi enabled device including computers, games, TV, etc.

The most complicated sticker we developed is the Smart Sticker. The so-called smart meter, that electric companies have been installing all over the world, uses technology similar to WiFi in the cell phone but it produces more complicated signal interactions. We went through many variations and combinations of ratios between raw Shungite powder and the S4 Shungite powder and had to add the concept of geometry to the mix, in how the powder piles were placed. The Smart Stickers can be put inside either the fuse box without being stuck down, or you can simply stick it to the door of the fuse box or the side of the fuse box.

Shungite Powder in Resin

In the very second radio show that Walt and I were on together, a conversation we were having led Walt to the thought, "Ah, I know what I can do, I will add Shungite powder to resin." I recently heard a replay of that show and was stunned to realize how early in the game Walt had picked up such a critical quality of Shungite that it allowed us to create a variety of Shungite S4 resin products.

Resin begins as liquid plastic. Through trials, Walt was able to develop a way of adding Shungite powder to the resin. He would then take this mix and pour it into plastic molds. After hours of curing he would take out the resin pieces full of Shungite.

We have gone through a large number of different types of molds, from the type of material to make the mold to the design of the piece being created. Initially, we were using small diamond-shaped and heart-shaped pieces to add to bracelet designs. Then Walt created a larger diamond-shaped piece which could be made into pendants. As I was into magnetic therapy I asked him to put a magnet in a diamond-shaped piece and then drill it so I could make it into a bracelet. I am still wearing it, and it has been over four years.

Magnetic therapy has got to be done with caution. The magnetic field needs to flow in a specific way into your body. Done correctly it is healing, but if you reverse the field the results can have negative effects. For that reason, we did not pursue the magnetic bracelet.

However, Walt's mother suggested this Shungite Magnet would make an excellent refrigerator magnet. Well, I had a bunch of these things here at the house. I took one and I stuck it on my refrigerator. This refrigerator had a 3-pound brick of Shungite inside it and a ½ dozen different Shungite stickers on the outside. When I stuck that Shungite magnet on the refrigerator there was a massive change in the texture of the energy field being put out by the refrigerator. This is a 20-year-old refrigerator with no electronics in it. I had no concept of what just happened.

I played with that magnet for I cannot tell you how long. I even went and got more of them and started playing with those. I had seen Shungite do some magical things but this one was baffling. I had to study it. By that I mean I had to clear my head of anything related to figuring out what was happening and just record what I was feeling and seeing regarding the energies.

Shungite loves an energy field. It can be water running down a pipe. It can be a human thought. It can be the electric field coming off of your electric wires in your house. It can be a WiFi signal. And it can be a magnetic field and that changed the game.

SHUNGITE S4 MAGNETS

ENERGY: Electric - Shungite - Quantum - Magnet

The problem I was having with the refrigerator's energy field hinged on the fact that there was no WiFi associated with the refrigerator. Prior to putting the magnet on the refrigerator I had not detected any bad energy. So why was there such a dramatic change in what I was feeling after the Shungite magnet was applied? And then I had the "ah ha" moment. There was actually no need to attenuate the signal as that had already happened with the stickers on the outside. What happened as a result of the magnet was an expansion, enhancement, and essentially an increase in the force of the energy field associated with the refrigerator. The electric energy was in the refrigerator. Even though we were using one small magnet, the electric and magnet fields combined with the Shungite field had resulted in the combined fields now being fueled by the quantum field. What essentially was happening was that the electric system and that little magnet had combined with the Shungite field powered by the quantum field to create a dynamic torsion field.

A torsion field is a donut shaped field of energy and is an extremely common form of energy. In fact, the human bioelectromagnetic energy field is in the shape of a torsion field.

We also find torsion fields in pyramids. In the 3D reality, energy follows geometry. The unique geometric structure of a pyramid in and of itself creates a torsion field inside the structure. It is a torsion field that is behind the seemingly magical properties of a pyramid.

The torsion field found in the pyramid extends from the top to the bottom. A torsion field in a square (or rectangle like a refrigerator) will eventually situate itself in the top 15% of the square – like near the ceiling of a room. The torsion field created by the electric, magnetic, Shungite, and quantum fields retains a dynamic and self-perpetuating motion that permeates the entire refrigerator. It Is contained within the refrigerator and it surrounds the refrigerator, radiating many feet into the environment.

It was the dynamic torsion field bleeding into the environment that I had felt. Shungite had just taught me something else. Whereas you can attenuate a signal to make it biocompatible, the signal still exists. It is a force of energy that is not natural, whether being radiated by the electric system or by electronic devices.

When merged with the Shungite field, these unnatural energy signals act as fuel to intensify the Shungite field. By putting a Shungite magnet on the refrigerator, the refrigerator becomes an energy device and the source of a very healing Shungite – electric – magnetic – quantum energy field radiating into the kitchen and surrounding rooms. And because you do not have to recharge or clean the Shungite magnet, its healing energy is always present.

This new information sent Walt on a mission to determine what kind and size of magnet should be used. When we finally decided we had a "final product", we sent samples off to friends who are energy sensitive. Based upon their observations it was decided to offer refrigerator magnets in the Internet store. It was many weeks later that people began realizing the food inside the refrigerator was tasting better and lasting longer. In fact one of the problems we had initially was that the refrigerators got too cold and some of us had vegetables frozen. We now warn people to watch that Shungite refrigerators do not get too cold.

The food lasting longer and tasting better mirrors reports of what happens in a pyramid and can be linked to the properties found in torsion fields. If the refrigerators got colder without a change of the thermostat, we surmised the refrigerator was working better or more efficiently. Less electricity was being used to keep the refrigerator cold and the Freon in the refrigerator – the gas that creates the cold – was undoubtedly a better grade with the addition of the refrigerator magnet. In addition to efficiency being seen with an addition of a Shungite magnet to a refrigerator, there was also measurable electric savings.

Shungite and Efficiency

When we were developing the magnets, Walt sent me a 3 inch tall resin dolphin with three magnets in it. As I knew my Aunt Peg, at 88 years old, would not be up for a science lesson in Shungite, I figured the least I could do was give her the dolphin, which would radiate her kitchen and a good portion of the house with Shungite healing energy. And by healing, I mean an energy that will balance the bioelectromagnetic field of the human body to promote physical health.

My aunt is legally blind and has developed a memory to keep track of her bills. After three months with the dolphin refrigerator magnet she said to me over the phone, "I've been meaning to tell you I think my electric bill has gone down since I put the Shungite magnet on the refrigerator."

"Well how much do you think you've saved," I asked.

Peg hesitated while doing some calculations in her head and then replied, "It must be 1/3 cheaper. Yes, the electric bill is down by 1/3."

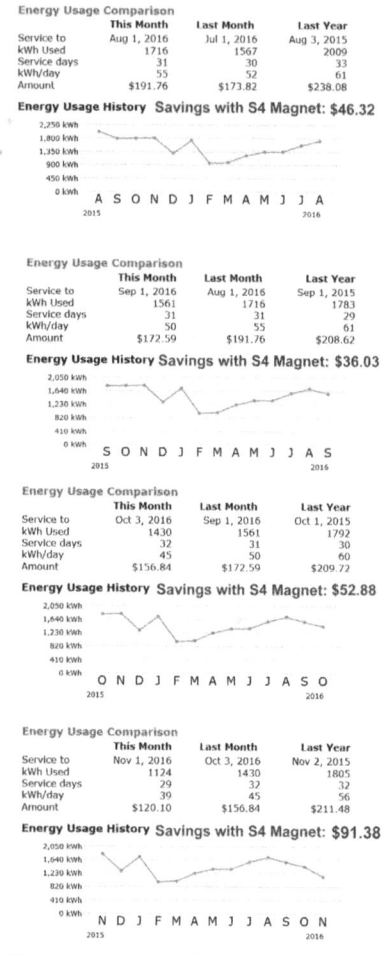

Home savings in a Shungite Environment

So I reported back to Walt my Aunt's observations and added, "We have to figure out the energy savings associated with the Shungite magnets."

In and around the same time, Walt did a series of experiments that proved if you put a Shungite magnet on the natural gas pipe going into your house, you will use less gas. He also got better gas mileage by adding the Shungite magnet to his automobile. We can understand this as being a result of Shungite detoxifying petrochemical fuels making them more efficient, and perhaps the Freon gas in the refrigerator was going through the same cleansing, resulting in more efficiency. And because the Freon was more efficient there was less electricity used? Nope, that did not seem to mesh.

You guessed it, Walt figured out another way to test everything. What he discovered was that the electric usage decreased when you put a Shungite magnet on the refrigerator or any other electrical device. We will discuss this more later. For now, the point I want to make is we now had proof that Shungite was doing something. And by proof I mean the kind "mainstream science" likes to see. Comparisons of electric bills showed Shungite did save you money.

I met Walt Silva in September 2014. The stickers and the magnets were brought into the inventory in early 2015. When the Internet store had opened in May 2014 the only products offered were the nuggets and pendants that were wire wrapped. Nuggets, stickers and magnets fall into the category of environmental protection. What we are going to discuss now are the pendants that provide individual protection.

INDIVIDUAL PROTECTION - PENDANTS

When the Gaia's Gift internet store opened, in addition to nuggets, there were wire-wrapped pendants available. I had been wrapping gems and minerals since 1992 and by the time I met Walt, I had wrapped over 500 Shungite pendants for both humans and animals. And then Walt explained to me what these little energy devices were and how they worked.

Shungite's ability to conduct electricity is a proven attribute. But the direction of energy flow I could detect was not electricity. To me it was just energy. Same thing with the wires that had an energy flowing that also had directionality. But in working with the nugget I made sure energy flow in both the wire and nugget was in the same direction. Walt explained the energy I was detecting is called by many names including Orgone, Prana, Chi and The Life Force.

Wire-wrapped Pendants

When orgone flows through both the wire and the Shungite nugget, the orgone is enhanced by the Shungite energy field being fueled by the Quantum Field connection. The resulting energy field expands to envelop the entire bioelectromagnetic field of the individual or pet. The bioelectromagnetic field refers to the entire intricate energy field comprised of chakras, nadias, meridians and other energy systems. The Shungite Wire Pendant brings stability to the bioelectromagnetic system that results in grounding and repairing the circuits.

When the individual encounters a toxic environment,

whether EM/WiFi, chemical, or radiation with the anti-life, negative rotation, the Shungite Wire Pendant continually adjusts the bioelectromagnetic field to bring back stability, as the toxic energy field is attenuated to become biocompatable.

S4 Shungite Resin Pendants

Walt's S4 Shungite Powder ended up in resin, which is a liquid plastic poured into molds that cures to become whatever shape the mold is. The success of the S4 formula in the S4 Stickers prompted us to see what other products could be made to hold the powder. From the second radio show we had, Walt knew the powder could be used in the resin.

Using a diamond-shaped mold and the S4 Shungite mix powder, Walt created a resin diamond that he could drill to allow a wire connection to be made. Thus, the creation of the S4 Shungite Resin Pendant. With the S4 now in pendant form, the EM/WiFi signals being encountered were being attenuated before entering the toroidal field of the bioelectromagnetic frequencies of the human, animal or plant.

While the WiFi signals are biocompatable regarding spin, the force of those signals still hits the individual's bioelectromagnetic field. These pendants do not stabilize and balance the individual's energy field as well as the wire wrapped pendants.

I began recommending that an individual wear both pendants. If I had to choose between the two, I would choose the wire wrapped pendant. This pendant's energy field works better with 3-D energy. Yes, it balances and stabilizes the bioelectromagnetic field, and also enhances physical healing in the form of quantum proto-energy.

Structured Shungite Pendant

Walt decided to put a bunch of nuggets in a tumbler thinking it might be a better way to get Raw Shungite Powder. A tumbler uses sand-like grit to polish stones as they are rotated in the tumbler and that would not work. So he put a bunch of screws and metal pieces into the tumbler. He sent the Shungite nuggets to me. It did not work for creating powder as the Shungite just became pounded, not broken up into powder.

However, the nuggets had definitely been changed. This energy is laser like and it fluctuates through the entire frequency spectrum. It has been suggested this pendant works with Reiki energy. Personally I have never been drawn to Reiki, nor am I drawn to this pendant. I do not recommend it unless YOU feel drawn to it. If you are, then that is what you should work with. We call it "Structured Shungite" because the change is at the molecular level where the molecules line up more uniformly, creating a different energy pattern.

Cosmic Silver Saturated Shungite Pendant

It was not until Derek Condit joined the team that we were able to take Walt's pounded nuggets to an entirely different level of energy. Derek used high grade silver instead of metal and created Silver Saturated Shungite

Pendants. We added "Cosmic" to the title to indicate the powerful connection to the Quantum Field created by pounded silver-impregnated Shungite.

This energy will both attenuate WiFi signals completely, while stabilizing the bioelectromagnetic fields.

As of the end of 2018, Gaia's Gift has expanded our Shungite products to include laminated stickers, Shungite Spirals/Pyramids/Pendulums, advanced energy devices and a line of Shungite honey/beeswax products. But the basics of how Shungite works and the products we had from very near the beginning are what most of the Customer Testimonials are based upon. And what did the customers say?

BASIC SHUNGITE PRODUCTS

Nuggets are used primarily for water purification and gifting to Nature to create the Shungite World Grid. The Bucky Bag contains smaller nuggets than recommended for drinking water.

Bucky Bag

All three basic pendants will attenuate electric signals. When WiFi signals are encountered, the S4 Resin Pendant attenuates the signal. The Wire-Wrapped Pendant balances the bioelectromagnetic energy body. The Cosmic Silver Pendant is silver saturated and attenuates WiFi signals and balances the bioelectromagnetic energy body.

Wire-wrapped

S4 Resin

Cosmic Silver

There are three Shungite stickers. The Bucky Bandaid works on electric systems, the S4 Sticker is used with electronic devices, and the Smart Sticker is put on fuse boxes. Magnets are used on refrigerators and other large appliances, cars, natural gas and oil systems.

S4 Magnets

Chapter 2

Testimonials - compiled by Jan Shaw

Shungite Bees

I just promised we were going to find out what our customers have reported. Our most important customers are the Honeybees. They have no preconceived notions of what Shungite is or what it does. The first they know about it is when someone puts three nuggets at the entrance to their hive. If Honeybees demonstrate enhanced health in a Shungite Environment, perhaps humans will be more receptive to studying Shungite for themselves.

To sum up what happened when honeybee hives were turned into Shungite Beehives between 20017 and 2019, three seasons of beekeeping resulted in:

> - over a million bees being produced each season. Each season began with only two starter hives and absolutely no chemicals were used;

> - no deaths attributable to ticks, mold, disease and there was no Colony Collapse.

For a full discussion of this topic, see Chapter 5. Shungite Beehives are now found worldwide with similar stunning results. The vast majority of these beehives do not use any chemicals whatsoever.

Customer Testimonials

The following is just a slice of the hundreds of testimonials given on Facebook, You Tube and verbally on radio shows or just by people reporting experiences. It was the customers' observations confirming our own that propelled the growth of the internet store. We decided to take a sampling from the "Customer Testimonials" that you can see at: https://www.cosmicreality.net/shungite-customer-comments

In 2014 I was miraculously led to finding Nancy Hopkins and Cosmic Reality Shungite. I read the information about EMF and WiFi radiation and how Shungite can protect against them. Holly, my Jack Russell was acting very nervous and uptight so I decided to get some Shungite nuggets and Bucky Bags. I put a Bucky Bag on the WiFi router and immediately felt a difference in the atmosphere in the house. It felt much calmer and Holly became much calmer too. I also put Shungite nuggets in my water and in the dog's water bowl. When I tasted the Shungite water it felt SO smooth by comparison to how it tasted before. Now I'm an advocate for Shungite and telling everyone about it. Thank you, Nancy, for introducing me to the miraculous Shungite!

- Jan S. 4/12/2014

Thank you, Nancy, for the gift of Shungite! As a gifted sensitive, I am very affected by EMF frequencies. I noticed immediately after having the Shungite in my home that the negative electromagnetic radiation was absorbed and transmuted into a positive charge. I became a REAL believer of Shungite when I came back from a 3-day vacation and observed the water in my vase to be crystal clear just sitting next to a few Shungite pieces! I know now why Shungite is called "medicine of the XXI century".

- Stephanie D. 5/29/2014

Thank you for educating and introducing my daughter and I to this amazing miracle rock. My experience is that I work under a cell phone tower and I never had an explanation for my constant headaches. Since having my Shungite, WOW! Not only do I feel great, but I also am not bloated like I was due to recent thyroid surgery, and my headaches are gone!!!!. My daughter, being the gifted sensitive child that she is, her experience was out of this world. She collects stones and rocks and she said that this is the one she was missing the whole time. She heals and cleans everything with it!!!

- Laura V. 5/29/2014

After listening to Nancy on a radio interview I ordered a Shungite pendant which I have worn every day for over a month now. I also placed 4 small pieces at the electrical meter on my house. Less than a week after the Shungite/meter placement we had a visitor stay with us for 3 days. The 2nd evening our visitor commented on how peaceful and serene our home felt to her. She raved about the energy present in our home. This woman is an energetic healing practitioner in her mid-70s and very sensitive to such energies. I also placed a small piece of Shungite in an aloe concentrate which I draw from and consume every morning. Over the past month, the piece has melted into a shiny smaller nugget. I'm getting Shungite'd and it feels good.

- Alan D. 6/13/2014

Shungite is very special and very powerful. I gave a pendant to my friends in school and they said that they feel a force field around them like a superhero! We have to do a lot of computer work in school and it gives us headaches and burns our eyes. We love our Shungite pendants because they help us to calm down and have fun on the computer. I want every teacher and student in my school to have one!

- Jordyn (Age 7) 6/14/2014

I have been using these Shungite stones for only a few days and all I can tell you is that something Good is Happening. I have been feeling down lately with a disease that has been difficult to deal with. I am actually feeling much better and I wanted to give you a 'testimonial' that they work! I wear this around my neck 24/7 and I put them in my water and my cat's water as well. Yesterday, they were dancing all around my lawn like it was the best day of their lives and today I have been feeling the same way. From my heart to yours, Nancy!

- Kristy K. 6/17/2014

I started using Shungite in my water and using it to water my plants and they went into this exponential growth spurt. They literally shifted into immediate plant growth and have not stopped. I've never seen anything like it!!!! Now I'm using the Shungite in water for my two pugs!

- Kimberlee 6/19/2014

I received my Shungite a couple of months ago..... and I have to say I was a total skeptic that it would do me any good whatsoever. My mind was mush, from all the drugs I was taking to keep my body working. I have Rheumatoid Arthritis, Fibromyalgia, Crohns Disease, Thyroid Disease, COPD and a host of other health problems that were all keeping me from living life.

After about a month, I (and my hubby) noticed I was thinking clearer. I was not so spaced out, and could actually hold a nice long conversation. The true test was when hubby let me balance our checkbook for the first time in several years and it was a success! As time passed I continued to drink my Shungite water and wear my pendants daily.

I am not kidding you... one day I just woke up feeling so good, I decided I would try to take a walk, just a short one, as I didn't want to overdo it and hurt like hell the following day. The next day, the same thing, I walked a wee bit farther than the day before and over the last few weeks, I have finally walked myself back up to an entire mile. You don't know how good this feels to move like this again! I have a lot of weight to drop from sitting so much and so many steroids and walking will help me do it quickly!!! Before I broke down and got "sick" I walked 3 miles daily without fail.

I FIRMLY in my heart believe if not for the Shungite, my brain would still be in a fog and I would not be having the clarity or energy I have. I have done nothing different other than purchasing the Shungite and using it!! Please, please, believe me when I say TAKE THE CHANCE and make that purchase! I was at the end of my ropes and so desperate.

I will never be without my pendants ... and I will continue to keep moving and walking... and never give up trying to get back to my normal life!!! THANK YOU NANCY, THANK YOU, for the quick & courteous delivery and for providing me with a stone that is so magical, so unbelievably unique that I can hardly believe it myself!!!!!!

I should also mention that I have been able to cancel FIVE (that's right 5!!!) doctor's appointments and I am now going to slowly try to eliminate some of my meds on my own. I really think the Shungite has saved me so much money already in medical bills. This is yet another day when I am feeling like a spring chicken again.. nothing is hurting or aching and I am mentally clear... this is amazing!

- Deb J. 7/24/2014

I received my Shungite Earrings and Bucky Bags on 7/7/14. I immediately put the earrings on and instantly felt my head do a subtle spin, like a 180, a shift. Then I remembered being told that I would immediately notice a difference upon putting the earrings on. I placed my Bucky Bags on my cable boxes and later I noticed the energy was mellow – energetic, but mellow and calm. I then decided that I would order more so I gave a couple of the Bucky Bags away since I wanted to share. So, I no longer had one in my office and after about a week I actually starting feeling sick and experienced nausea while sitting at my computer. My second order arrived and I definitely noticed a difference with the energy again. I know first hand that Crystals, Stones, and Rocks have properties that do shift the energies and I totally recommend Shungite. I just love the vibration and I am grateful that it came my way.

- Melissa A. 8/4/2014

Thank you, Nancy, for gifting me the awesome pieces of Shungite!! They all arrived right on time!! I was truly suffering since the local electric/gas companies installed all "Automated" meters in every unit in my apartment complex. Since the installation of "Automated" meters, my legs ached, my face was burning, and I had trouble sleeping.

On February 21st my left knee, ankle, and foot were extremely painful. I soaked in an Epsom salt bath, massaged with essential oils, even did mild stretching, but the pain still continued!! I took a little walk and checked my mailbox - what a very pleasant awesome Shungite surprise!! I I immediately put on the Shungite pendant. I started to feel a relaxing shift in energy around me. Within the span of thirty minutes, all my pain was gone!!

I placed the Bucky Bandaids on the electric meter, and cordless phone and placed a Bucky Bag on my computer surge protector. As for the Shungite nuggets, they are in my bottled water.

Just from the results of the Shungite Pendant, alone, I know all will work just fine!! I can finally get a good night's sleep!! Thank you again, Nancy. Your Assistance, Compassion, and Empathy Are Greatly Appreciated!!

- B. Marie H. 2/22/2015

I just feel right with the Shungite around my neck. When I first put the Bucky Bag on my WiFi, my dad's coughing stopped, and we don't cough as much. I feel happier in general and don't feel as depressed anymore. Shungite is real.

- Shaan 2/26/2015

    I would like to start by saying thank you to Nancy for being so kind and welcoming. I love the Shungite I got from you guys. I wear a pendant every day and meditate with my Shungite brick and I'm also working with my purity spiral. I drink Shungite water every day and I can't drink water any other way now - I'm spoiled because it tastes so good! I also have my Bucky Bandaids on my phones. I honestly feel so much more in balance and I feel healthier. Some of the health problems I had before Shungite have simply just gone away. At first, it did take about a week for my body to adjust as I'm energy sensitive, but I knew from my research and listening to Nancy that this is normal and will pass, as it did and now after about 6 months or more of having Shungite in my life I feel great and want to tell everyone!!!! Thank you all so much. Love, light and Shungite!!

- Kathy B. 2/27/2015

    I wanted to give you some feedback about Shungite. My sister lives in Sweden and after talking to her about Shungite she ordered a bunch because she has a lot of wifi energy in the house, plus her kids have to have laptops in school and are bombarded with WiFi. Sweden is a very new world order traumatized country. It's almost cashless and microchips are being promoted.
    Anyhow, I spoke to my sister yesterday and she told me how her kids feel better, no headaches, waking up in the morning with more energy and they feel more

harmonious. And it also helps my sister who has carpal tunnel syndrome. Working as a dental hygienist holding vibrating tools puts her in pain. She goes to sleep with pain and wakes up with it. Well, guess what helps her!!! Shungite!!! She noticed yesterday how she has been painless since she put Shungite all over the house and on herself. She is ordering more! I Thought I'd let you know. Thank you Shungite angel, keep spreading the love!

One more thing...My shower head used to collect mildew and I used to wipe it off all the time and it used to come back. After I taped Shungite onto the water generator that runs the cold water and the hot water to the apartment there is no more mildew on my shower head!!

- Robin 4/21/2015

I wanted to share a few more things about the Shungite I am using (I am buying it only from you). I am specifically using your raw uncut "nuggets" for the following experiments:

Using silver wire 98% pure (the kind used in making jewelry) I am stringing together 3 separate pieces end-to-end and attaching them to my little Honda Civic (experimenting with one grouping inside the passenger area, and another grouping attached to the engine block). Using white hemp string I am stringing together 3 separate pieces end-to-end, and attaching them to hang from the interior top inside my refrigerator. I have found this to prolong the freshness of my organic produce and everything else I keep in the fridge in very excellent condition for a prolonged period of time. Example: My fresh kale, bell peppers, etc., used to only last up to two weeks, whereas now they are lasting up to a month. This is great news for me because as I had been experimenting with lowering my intake of food to one to one and a half meals a day (but of very good quality food only) due to finances and also to feeling that I didn't need as much food as before.

Again using only the raw uncut nuggets, I have used surgical cloth tape to apply an individual Shungite nugget to an area of an unsightly scar (it probably should have been stitched, but at the time I just let it heal on its own which it did but it left a rather bulky unsightly scar). After leaving the Shungite attached for a week, the scar tissue has flattened and receded much closer within the epidermis and feels much better too.

Then after reading Patti Conklin's book, "God Within", and her saying that rage and anger reside often within the 7th thoracic vertebra (resulting in extreme pain in that location), although I didn't feel like I had a lot of rage and anger, but considering the possibility of subconscious rage and anger, I decided to try taping a Shungite stone at the 7th vertebra, then also added one at the very last lumbar vertebra, and one at the mid-cervical vertebra. I also left these there for a week, then a 2nd week, and then a 3rd week. I have noticed a significant positive change on so many levels.

Then I noticed anywhere I had any pains or congestion (for instance in the groin lymphatic areas), I would apply an individual Shungite stone with the surgical tape and leave it for up to a week. Each time, the congestion and/or pain would completely resolve. Oddly at this point, I then noticed congestion/discomfort from my lymphatic area up in the armpit area (right side). I applied one Shungite stone to that area for a week, and again, this resolved within a week of its application.

If any congestion/pain returns in any area, I simply repeat the procedure again.

For my drinking/cooking water, I use three separate Shungite stones in a stainless steel pot that I always boil my water in that I use for making all my tea, cooking food with, etc. and perform a blessing over it. I have done a test where I taste water prepared this way and then without any Shungite/blessing. The difference in the taste, weight and 'feel' of the water is extremely different from my subjective observation. To me, the water even smells different. I much prefer the Shungite/blessing water.

As I say, I am using the word "experimentation" on purpose because I honestly also do a lot of prayer and meditation along with the application of the Shungite, and these are not controlled experiments (no control group, just me and my truly subjective observations).

Last, I ordered a Bucky bag and the Shungite pieces are fairly small, so I selected two fairly similar shaped pieces, wrapped them with silver wire and fashioned my own very small Shungite earrings. (I did this because I was ordering the Shungite nuggets and economizing - you have made some beautiful earrings, but I am really on a budget right now, so I made my own small ones). You shared that wearing the earrings will aid your pineal gland. I figure wearing a piece of Shungite wrapped in my hair bun atop my head, along with the Shungite earrings, would create a triangle grid which would be very helpful. I again have been experimenting with this also and it really does subjectively help strengthen and aid me in many ways.

Nancy, thank you again so much for all the information you share via your interviews and books. I wanted to take the time to share what I have been doing with the Shungite in the hopes that perhaps it may be of some small help to you and others. I hope this finds you well, and again, I am so grateful for the Shungite access via you. Thank you for all you do.

PS: I also use the Bucky Band-Aids on my laptop, work PC, other electrical items that stay on like CD/radio player, etc. and also notice a difference in the cell phone temperature improvement.

- 5/24/2015

Hello-where to begin. Three years ago depression set in – it's a long story. This set me on a mission-quest. Once upon a time, I was very peaceful - mostly. I've scoured over at least one hundred hours of YouTube videos looking for the solution to how to connect more strongly to source. So I tried everything from tapping, which was so so, EMDR which was better, NLP which was so so the Havening technique which was not bad and many more. Then I came upon Dr. Eric Pearl's Reconnective healing. I watched the demo videos, read the book and experimented feeling the frequencies for five hours a day for several days and wow this was a four-star day for three days, then of course I crashed. Then I found the Infinity wave and from this, it would seem I discovered true nonduality and even the Christ consciousness in that I was free from any obstructions and was connected to the best intrinsic value of each moment.. then I crashed again. Then I found myself watching Eric Pearl's video again about Moldavite and then I got not one or two but three specimens. Again, wow, and from there I stumbled upon Shungite.

I got five nuggets and didn't feel much right away, like the Moldavite, so I placed one in between each of my middle and forefinger and did a taffy energy pull until I began feeling the reconnective frequencies, and then I held the stones again and I started to feel a connection that was very organic. A very mellow peace came over me.

The next day or so later, I received two Shungite bracelets and the energy disks that are held in each hand - two elite Shungite necklaces and a Shungite pendant. Was wondering if you recommend wearing elite with raw Shungite, as you stated it was a different frequency. I put both bracelets on and the two pendants, felt the energy, then the next day I woke with the Shungite smack-down.

What, another crash? It is now evening - I had removed the bracelets earlier. Now I am wearing everything and feeling pretty good. Also, I have had really bad tennis elbow for six months. It seems a little better in just a few days. I also have a prostate issue and after reading other testimonies I am going to get creative for that issue and see what healing may occur. And I have heard different views about water purification. I think I will plop three Shungite stones into a mason jar and let it sit for three days and drink it.

- Joseph D. 8/26/2017

    I started researching Shungite to lessen the effect of 6 Smart Meters on the side of my apartment. I found my way to the Cosmic Reality website and ordered Shungite for the Smart Meters, WiFi, fridge, water heater, drinking water and some to make personal pendants. Thank you, Nancy, for sending one for the doggie, too!
    Needless to say, I jumped in deeply because it makes so much sense to surround my very sensitive family with something that can support us in feeling better. We have all been suffering for years with financial, physical and emotional disorders that seemed to be getting progressively after seeming to get better temporarily.

I heard that the Shungite, along with all it's attenuating of toxic energies, may clear away whatever is in the way of becoming a balanced human being. This is what I wanted... some deeper energetic helpers to move us along.

   I did experience right away what Nancy talked about - feeling supported in the face of extreme negativity. I was able to keep grounded in my love for the person and not what they were screaming at me. That really got my attention because it was a very different reaction from what I've previously had with this person. I had always been reacting emotionally at some point.

   Now after about 2 months of Shungite use, I have to say that I am of the portion of the population that is feeling a bit slam dunked...is it the Shungite, is it my thoughts about my reality, or both?! I don't really know. I don't think I'm that sensitive to energies, or if I am, I'm not that aware of it so possibly that's truer.

   Well, I have to say that issues are coming out of the woodwork for me to face. Veils are being lifted and I feel like I'm going through a huge identity crisis! It feels like the death of much of what I've believed to be true and there is also a sense of something else being born, although I'm still in that process.

   Is this the Shungite for sure? I don't know, but I did read some similar descriptions about it and I did think I'd much rather subscribe, at least consciously, to the flowery experiences of healing illnesses and feeling great.

   I continue to use it and I expect that in the next couple of months, I should have something new to say about it. Right now, I would advise you to hold onto your hat because you could be in for the ride of your life as Gaia's truth makes a stand in your reality.

   "Be safe" as Nancy says.

- Dela 9/13/2015

I used to hate going to certain stores because I would get such buzzing in my ears, the hairs on my neck would stand up, and I would get so dizzy. I always thought there must have been a lot of EMFs in these stores. I received my Shungite pendant on Monday and I couldn't wait to get it around my neck. On Wednesday I went to those certain stores to see if I felt any different. To my surprise, there was no buzzing in my ears, no hair standing up on my neck, and no dizziness. I am so grateful to Gaia for giving us the gift of Shungite. I must add I'm so grateful to you Nancy and Walt for making Shungite available to us at an affordable price. Blessings.

- 11/5/2015

Though I am very familiar with and have used Organite, Selenite and Green Kyanite quite a bit with good results, I had never heard of or used Shungite before. As soon as I received my delivery from you I placed the pieces of Shungite and the Bucky Bandaids/stickers in the various places that called for them.

I also started wearing the choker necklace with the Shungite pendant. I did not wear it consistently in the beginning but then started being drawn to wearing it to bed and also whenever I felt out of sorts. Finally, I got called to place the Shungite pendant on a long piece of hemp string where it hangs just between my heart chakra and solar plexus chakra. I am wearing it all the time now next to my skin under my clothes.

The Shungite pieces and Bucky Bandaids have been beneficial and the biggest benefit I have noticed is from

wearing my Shungite pendant all the time day and night. I feel much calmer & balanced and seem to even sleep deeper when wearing it as compared to when I didn't wear it. I absolutely love all my Shungite and most especially my Shungite pendant!
    Thank you again for such an amazing and helpful tool! Much Love,

- Deb R. 2/12/2016

    Since having Shungite on all of the WiFi systems in my office the energy feels so much lighter as before it was heavy and dense. We are more focused with clarity which in turn facilitates a positive environment of productivity. It has brightened up all operations and my clients are leaving feeling energized and happy.

- Dr, Evan J. H. 5/17/2016

    We own a Holistic Organic Wellness Center in Boca Raton and we love Shungite! We are adding it to all of our skin care blends and even putting the nuggets in our Ionix detox foot baths. We notice that the Shungite is pulling out more toxins from the body and aiding in faster healing. Shungite is enhancing the "energy" work we are doing in skin care for our clients. We also have the S4 Refrigerator Magnet and we did our own test and found that the spinach has been in our refrigerator for 3 weeks! By day 3 it should be wilted and it was still fresh. Our electric bill also went down almost $70 a month since having Shungite stickers on our systems and the magnet on our fridge.
    I also want to share another amazing Shungite

experience. So far I have experienced plants coming back to life, keeping my produce fresher longer, lowering my monthly FPL bill, and giving my skin care powders the most incredible texture.

We just had ANOTHER Shungite realization - our Water Alkalinizer machine would only bring water to an alkalinity of pH 8.7 but after placing a large Shungite specimen on top of the machine it is now bringing the water to an alkalinity of pH 9.2. I'm continuously blown away by this miracle mineral. Thank you Cosmic Reality Shungite!

- Stephanie C. 5/17/2016

Since I have been using Shungite in my healing work I've noticed it has given me greater clarity as a healer. It also sustains the work I do on my clients because it creates a force field of protection around them as they walk out into a toxic world of EMF radiation. I HIGHLY encourage all of my clients to get Shungite for themselves and their loved ones to keep them physically safe from EMF's and to feel more grounded and less stressed.

- Sherinata P. 6/2/2016

The first time I held Shungite I felt an electric current run through my heart like it was zapping me back to life. I felt alive for the first time in years---really HAPPY! I got my groove back :)

- Maria L. 6/2/2016

I bought the EMF/WiFi Home Protection Kit and since having Shungite S4 Stickers on all of our WiFi systems, S4 Magnet on Refrigerator and a Smart Sticker on our Smart Meter our used kilowatts on our energy bill went down 127kw and my electric bill went down $28.00 in ONE MONTH !!! Having a "Shungite Environment" is not only an investment in your families health but also in your pocket!

- Suzanne K. 6/2/2016

Thank you so much for my Shungite. I wanted to share that I have lost 5 lbs in one week and have done nothing different besides wearing my pendant, drinking the water, and have the S4 Stickers on my devices. Most importantly I stopped wearing my fit bit and I am sleeping so much better and have unlimited energy and focus! Please keep up the good work and spreading the word of Shungite to the world. Its been a game changer in our lives and we are grateful.

- Claire 6/2/2016

I started wearing the Shungite Pendant about one and a half weeks ago. Within 2 days I noticed an immediate shift in my consciousness. I felt so at peace with myself and everything around me. Feeling blissfully empowered is simply putting it mildly. I am no longer bothered by trivialities. Also the greatest shift was noticed in my partner. He seems so less anxious and distant, and is actually communicating in a much more loving way. The effect was miraculous! I intend to purchase more items for myself and family members. I Also used the magnet in my car and successfully completed a 600+ miles trip without any car trouble (as I was experiencing earlier). Thank you, Thank You, Thank You!

- Marjorie 6/26/2016

    Thank-you Nancy: I would like to share an experience I had with the Shungite stone. For as long as I can remember I have had insomnia. I would toss and turn for up to 3 hours before I finally fell asleep. My twin sister gave me a shungite pendant that she put around my neck. Immediately, that first night, I fell asleep and slept for 8 hours straight and when I awoke I felt very refreshed. I was thinking back about when I went to bed and I don't remember even thinking about anything, I just fell asleep.

    My mother was with me when I got the pendant from my twin sister (my mother lives with me I take care of her I am her caretaker). Her mood the next day was not a pleasant one so I stayed clear of her as much as I could that day. Then the following day I took her to Senior Citizen Center. When we got home her mood was even worse and my dogs started growling and barking at her as though she was a stranger. That was very odd to me because they have never done that before unless it was a stranger in my home. I was worried that my mother might have picked up an entity from somewhere because she is at a vulnerable stage in her life. She is 91 years old and her mind is not as sharp as it used to be.

    I took my mother outside and saged her. I asked her to stay outside while I saged the whole house and when I got to her room and started saging it, the sage started flaring out into sparks and burned small holes all over her pillowcase. I had never seen that happen before with sage, that worried me, and the hair on my arms stood up and I did not have a good feeling in her room. When I was through saging the house I went back into her room and the hair on my arms stood up again, so I saged her room once again but I was more aggressive with the chant that I used (whatever gave me that feeling in her room is no longer there).

    I have had this pendant for a week now and my mother's mood has changed dramatically like night and day. At first, after the whole house was cleansed and I spoke to my mother she was like a different person, someone that I did not know. That is a good thing because this new person is a sweetheart, someone I love to be around. There were days that I regretted the choice I made to have her move in with me, but those days are gone. I enjoy her company now.

    My twin sister ran across this Shungite stone by accident (or was it fate?). There are no accidents; it was meant to be. I used to have anxiety a lot and now I have none. I used to have insomnia and now I don't, I absolutely love this stone and I would recommend it to everyone. I actually have more stones on order to give them to family members. Thank you so much for putting the word out there Nancy Hopkins.

- Naomi Phillips 8/27/2016

    First I'd like to thank you immensely for these Shungite pieces. They are fantastic! I never heard about them, saw a few people I admire mention them, and did a little research, which is unlike me. I usually research things to death, but I had a good vibe. I was a little skeptical but open-minded going into the purchase and trial of the

Shungite pieces.

    Upon first receiving them, I felt they had a neutralizing and relaxing feel to them. Any anxious energy was very much dissipated as well as overly happy energy was dampened. As an empath, they help me so much dealing with other people's energy and even my own sometimes. By wearing or having these items on my person or near me, I have the ability to stay more objective more easily. As an empath, I had to strengthen my abilities to protect and identify others emotions vs my own, and on days when I'm tired, or just an off day, it's easy for that shield of awareness to come down. This Shungite gives me that extra edge to maintain objectivity when in the presence of others who have severe emotions and are projecting those emotions at me. The result is that the negative energy that I feel from others is less intense and it seems less likely to have the piercing ability it can have for people who really know how to project emotions onto me.

    I'm not a big believer in relying on items outside yourself for power or to achieve your goals. Everything you need is within you, however, having these items does help, as I said, they "give you an edge" or just extra help. I do not wear these daily all day, but I do wear them several times per week. I keep the pyramid between myself and my computer to help dissipate the energy released by the device onto my body.

    Once again, thank you so very much for these items. They appear to be made very solid and of good quality and workmanship. I will recommend them to friends, and also come back for gifts during the holidays! To Awakening!

- AG 6/8/2016

Two to four billion years ago something hit the Earth and landed in Russia near the Finnish border. Made of carbon it looks like coal but doesn't burn. There's a lake nearby that contains pure water, so much so that it is drinkable. People take containers of it home. It is near a town named Shunga so it is called Shungite. Its molecules are in the shape of a geodesic dome so they were named Fullerenes after Buckminster Fuller.

Shungite reverses the direction of water to its natural flow. In the Northern Hemisphere, water flows in a clockwise direction. Toxins that are added to it flow in a counter-clockwise direction. All electrics are set to move in the same direction, against Nature. Shungite changes that. Add three small nuggets of Shungite to a gallon of water and the water changes direction while the toxins, added by the city to tap water, are dissolved. They aren't absorbed by the Shungite, they are dissolved when the water changes directions, which also adds antioxidants to the water.

The people at cosmicreality.net have discovered that the powder is more potent than a nugget. and mixed with silver is even stronger. A small sticker with powdered Shungite is used for electrical devices. They are called Bucky Bandaids. S4 Stickers with silver saturated Shungite are used for electronics. Put one on your WiFi router and it changes directions to move in a clockwise direction, thereby eliminating the radiation that is making you sick, possibly without your knowing it.

I thought my eyes were hurting from looking at the monitor. They don't hurt anymore so it was the radiation that was causing it. I read a book yesterday at HotFreeReads and barely had eyestrain at the end of it. A few days ago I would have taken days to finish it because my eyes would have been bothering me so much.

I put a small Bucky Bandaid on my refrigerator. It's an energy saver but seems to run all the time, making too much noise. With the bandaid on the door, I've had to turn down the coldness dial twice. It is now set at 2 ½ and will probably have to be lowered again. It doesn't run all the time anymore and is quieter when it does. And the produce...wow! it stays fresher longer. My diet is Macrobiotic so I use lots of fresh veggies. I found a small piece of broccoli in a plastic bag that had gotten overlooked for several days. I expected it to be covered with black gooey stuff, but it looked like the day I put it in there. When I walked barefoot by the fridge I could feel the hot air blowing over my feet. Now I have to bend over and use my hand to feel the air, which is very low, and just barely warm. My fridge will last forever at this rate.

WiFi was bothering me so much I had to unplug it. I don't have it hooked up again but I expect I'll be able to use it again. And my iPad. I have S4 stickers on the iPad and laptop. I wear a pendant and I can walk without holding to furniture in my house. It was better when I unplugged the WiFi but is much better now with the Shungite.

You can put 3 larger nuggets on the water pipe that goes into your house and all the water going in will be pure. Cosmic Reality and Walt Silva have developed many things on their own for their company. They just want to get this stuff into everyone's life. There are stickers for your car that will make it run better, getting better gas mileage. Every sticker you put on something will make the motor run better and last longer. There is even something for a Smart Meter. I sent Walt an email giving some info about what I was experiencing. He had just developed a new kind of pendant that was very powerful. He said he had an instinct to help me and thought this would work. He had to send me the one he was using. Apparently just took it off his neck and sent it to me. These are good people that care about humanity and the planet.

- Lorey 9/12/2016

PS: UPDATE ON MY REFRIGERATOR:

I have lowered the cold dial again. It is now set at #2. Just 2! And it's working fine.

The ice trays - usually when I empty an ice tray, I have to twist the plastic tray a few times to get all the ice out. Some of the cubs come out in one piece but there is much splintering of ice all over, and several broken cubes. Also, some ice sticks to the tray and won't come out. That has changed dramatically. I gave the tray a twist and every cube fell out intact. Not a splinter of ice anywhere and the tray was clean as a whistle. Perfect cubes.

I wanted to check how the water would freeze on #2 so I filled the tray and put it in the freezer again. I forgot to look at it for three hours but it was frozen hard. I don't know how long it actually took to freeze but I can live with whatever it is.

Now, the air coming from the vent that cools the motor is barely coming out and it is barely warm. That means the motor is just getting warm so very little air is necessary to cool it. The electric current isn't being forced to run backward, then run harder to do its job, while the fan must run on high to try to keep it cool. Can you imagine what a Bucky Band-aid would do for a lawnmower? And a leaf-blower?!

I have heard from folks that this is one of those things that is too good to be true. I can understand that kind of thinking, but this one really is true. Absolutely.

- Lorey 9/22/2016

I used to have horrible hot flashes during the night, which would always wake me up, and then I'd lie there twitching, wondering if I would ever fall back to sleep again. And of course, I wouldn't, just because I'm focusing on falling back asleep. Anyway, I've been wearing my Shungite to bed - what an amazing gift! I haven't had this much sleep in years! Thank you! Seriously! I've been telling everybody about it.

- Linda D. 10/29/2016

I was experiencing excruciating pain on my body from a car accident. I held three Shungite nuggets in my left hand a few hours before I went to sleep and they worked overnight as the pain in my left hand was tremendously reduced compared to the rest of my body aches. This was my first test using Shungite after someone had given it to me. Everyone's state of consciousness can be different after experiencing a traumatic event. The Shungite was a tool that assisted me to go inside to ask for maximal help in my recovery. Thank You Cosmic Reality Shungite.

- Dan R. 10/29/2016

I have been amazed at the power of this stone! I was having severe migraines and fatigue, and after drinking the Shungite water, wearing it, and having the S4 stickers on my WiFi devices... I feel so much better! I have worked with a lot of Shungite in the past as I sell crystals and minerals. Nothing has been as energetically charged as the raw Shungite from you guys. Now I understand why you call it the "Gift from Gaia". I am grateful to be a part of this sacred mission to get Shungite to the masses. It is truly a miracle stone!

- Healing and Crystal Therapy 10/29/2016

    I have been wearing my pendant for over a month now and placed nuggets all over my home. I must say, I feel for the most part, that negativity has been minimized if not removed from my life. How I react and think is calmer, more positive and optimistic. Overall my outlook is more positive, calm and balanced. I am pleased with my Shungite. Thank you, Nancy and the Shungite gang!

- Brenda N. 12/26/2016

    I have made a breakthrough that has surprised me. First, I am chemically sensitive so Shungite doesn't work immediately for me. I have to leave the nuggets in the water for 36 hours for it to be drinkable for me.
    So, I was choosing some organic food, which is all I can eat, at Trader Joe's and mistakenly grabbed a couple of bags of shredded cabbage that wasn't organic. I didn't realize it till I was home. I didn't know what to do with it but realized that if Shungite can remove the chemicals from water, why can't it do that for food? Especially small pieces of food. The cabbage was shredded to about 1/4 in.
    I dumped one of the packages into a container, covered it with Shungite water, and for good measure, dropped in 3 nuggets, covered it, and set it in the fridge. On the third day I took it out, drained the water and rinsed it with fresh Shungite water, dried it, ran it through the Cuisinart with some onion and carrot. Then mixed it all

together with Vegenaise, and boy, was it good! No chemicals at all!

So I did the same with the second bag of cabbage, but when I got it dry on the third day, I had fried cabbage. So good and chemical free!

- Lorey 1/19/2017

I put a Bucky Bandaid sticker on my fridge and turned it down by increments to #2. It used to make a loud pop when it started and stopped and the motor was quite loud. When I put the Bucky ball on it, the sound was lowered and I turned it down slowly to #2. It was still very cold so I wondered if I could turn it down a bit more.

I turned it down a small amount. This is when a strange thing happened. The sound it had made before - the original loud sound and the lowered sound - were alike, the difference was in volume. Now the sound changed. Actually changed! It sounds more like a hum now, really a different sound completely. I think the fridge has finally been normalized, that is, it has reached the harmonic hum that it should have been making all the time because it is finally running at peak efficiency.

At first, I would check to see if it was running as it was so quiet. And it runs even less frequently now than before I lowered the number to less than 2. Everything is cold or frozen as it should be. And no more pops when it starts and stops. What are they doing to make machines do the things they do? I know, they're made to break down or quit running completely. I am constantly amazed at this stuff called Shungite.

- Lorey 11/3/2017

The teachers and I were recently introduced to the crystal Shungite. At first, I was a bit skeptical of its energy and healing powers but decided to buy a home kit and give it a try. I cannot say enough great things about it. My fruits and veggies never lasted longer and taste so fresh and my electric bill is lower.

- Susana R. 3/29/17

When we bought our property, it came with a mama cat that took us 6 years to catch. We were able to catch her kittens and get them fixed, but it took us a long time to stop the kitten factory at its source, so by the time we finally got mama kitty fixed, we had 8 cats and I liked to say, very few gophers.

Well suddenly, our cats start disappearing. About a week after I put 9 good sized pieces of Shungite in our bird bath, one of their sources of water. Over a period of a few weeks our cats slowly began to disappear, one by one, till now we just have 3 left. We think perhaps a fox got them. At first, I couldn't understand it, Shungite is the great protector, right? My intention in putting Shungite in their water was so that all the local wildlife could have an energized water source, not kill off our kitties!

Then a few evenings ago, as I was sitting near my birdbath I was suddenly taken by all the birds that were around, bluebirds, robins, sparrows, titmice, and then it hit me, I put the Shungite in the BIRD BATH, and now birds are flourishing. A balance has come to our property. Our feral cats had much longer lives with the care and love we gave them, and now, they've moved on, and it's time for the bird and lizard populations to flourish amidst all the native plants I've put in. I believe Shungite brought a healthy balance to our property.

- VV 5/9/2017

I love Shungite - that is an easy one for me. It's already working wonders in a few hours. I was temporarily dealing with pain in my joints in the higher limbs and it seems the pain has left my body. This Shungite necklace is a beauty. What a beautiful healing stone.

- Kelly A. 5/17/2017

Love these rocks! Definitely an amazing energy for all my clients and friends that are energy sensitive. You need this! I own a salon and I put three nuggets on my hot water tank which is an on-demand water heater. It used to jump around and get hot and then go back to cold and now it just stays the right temperature! Yay!

- Julie E. 5/17/2017

I got a new phone and it didn't have an S4 Sticker on it. Three days later my ear was really hurting. The doctor said my inner ear drum was swollen and I had a thing called "tinnitus". I needed to go on antibiotics. My mom realized this was the same ear that I hold my phone on to talk. Now we really understand the power of the S4 Sticker on my phone. I never want to be in pain like that again! Thank you so much Cosmic Reality Shungite.

- Corinne K. 5/17/2017

While I was recovering in the hospital after my surgery a good friend introduced me to the healing stone Shungite and CosmicReality.net, the company whose mission is to raise awareness of this ancient sacred mineral and also make it available to everyone. We live in an increasingly toxic environment. Shungite shields you and all living things from electro-magnetic and WiFi radiation. I've been wearing a copper coiled pendant for the last month and my healing has been highly accelerated. I also use the Shungite stickers on all electronic devices in my home and drink water "on the rocks". Educate yourself about this growing threat as we continue to fill our planet with harmful radiation and toxic metals and chemicals. This isn't a conspiracy theory - it's a scientifically agreed understanding. Just read the warnings in the fine print in the manuals for your phones, computers, routers and other gadgets. And consider using Shungite to protect yourselves, your family, your plants, and animals.

- Jeff S. 5/17/2017

I haven't taken off my Shungite necklace since I got it in December. I am also using a Shungite toothbrush and I have started drinking Shungite infused water. It has helped me through extreme stress, protected me from colds and viruses and improved my gum issue so much that I am not needing a scheduled extraction! So Grateful for Shungite.

- Shynin L. 5/17/2017

Results from having an S4 Sticker on my cell phone, computer & WiFi router: I sleep better. I feel extremely energized. I am a writer and I noticed that my focus and creativity have increased. No more procrastination in my daily tasks and they are done with minimal effort. My friends have noticed that my eyes have lit up and are smiling. I AM HAPPY.

- Anon 5/17/2017

When I first encountered Shungite I noticed the energy when I held it in my hand. Recently I purchased a Shungite hoop. I wanted this because I have a sterling silver necklace. I have another pendant but it needs a string wire. I find this inconvenient for showering, etc, and I like my silver necklace.

Wow, what a difference! Boom! I noticed the energy went up a gear. I suddenly had a feeling of energy around my head that has continued ever since I made silver contact with the Shungite hoop. It felt like I lit up like a Christmas tree.

What I noticed with the silver Shungite vs the Shungite on its own is that it seems to be providing an additional layer of protection. I notice with Shungite that I am aware of negativity although its effects are nullified. This can be unsettling and can cause consternation - a "Shungite smackdown"! However, the silver interacting with the Shungite feels much nicer.

I summarize as follows:
> Shungite on its own - negative energy/radiation hits your body but you can adjust, it negates negative effects, it can feel unsettling
> Silver with Shungite - negative energy/radiation doesn't even hit your energy body, it

negates negative effects, it feels comfortable

Also, I have noted that the silver on my chain is starting to come off and coat the inside of my Shungite hoop, interesting. It's like silver powerfully interacts with Shungite, perhaps it creates an even stronger connection to the quantum zero-point field. Whereas I get immense benefit from Shungite on its own, silver is so much nicer and you get none of the "Shungite smackdown". I know that with your S4 (silver-saturated) stickers you have noticed a stronger effect on all the benefits of Shungite.

- Jamie 7/2/2017

I have been living in a Shungite environment now for about 2 months. Yes, more energy but the most amazing thing that I realized is that I no longer have carpal tunnel syndrome! When I had chelation therapy to remove heavy metals back in 2004-2005, the carpal tunnel went away then as well which I thought was very strange. However, it came back, probably in about 2010, and got progressively worse again. I'm 69 and have been typing almost daily (still do) for about 47 years. That's my validation that this stuff really works and I'm keeping it around forever!

- Ginger C. 7/10/2017

POW-ER-FUL! I just received my stickers and magnets. While I could feel the vibrations through the packaging, it really hit me, in a good way, when I opened the envelope. My cats pounced on the contents and wanted to roll in it. Everything is in place and I feel the positive energy already. Can't wait to see the wonderful effects. Thank you all for sharing this Shungite!

- Leann 8/3/2017

The last colonoscopy I had three years ago I had polyps and lesions that needed to be removed resulting in scar tissue. Today I had my colonoscopy and the doctor was shocked to see that my colon was completely clear of any lesions including scar tissue. The doctor says this never happens, especially with my family history of colon issues. No coincidence here. I have been living in a Shungite environment and drinking the water for almost three years. I got my health back with this miracle mineral. My autoimmune issues have also been eradicated. Thank you Cosmic Reality Shungite.

- Sara 8/7/2017

I placed a magnet in my car after my last fill-up. according to the miles, I should be at the ½ way mark. instead, I'm at the 3/4 mark. Go Shungite!

- Leann 8/16/2017

My boyfriend has been a non-believer of anything esoteric (including religious). Everything that happened he could "explain" away. On a particularly grueling work week, he was having body-crippling muscle spasms. This is a young guy in great shape. I handed him a Shungite sphere and they stopped. He got up, collected another sphere and slept with them in his socks. Ha! He now carries Shungite with him almost all the time. Also, I would directly attribute to the stone a result that he couldn't explain away - he has begun channeling. This is a powerful awakening for a frat boy in the Bible Belt. (Absolutely no disrespect to the Bible or any religion.) The stones have had nothing miraculous happen as of yet for me, but again I have directly witnessed what they can do.

- Caroline B. 9/17/2017

I love my Shungite rubber mat!!!! I sleep on it every night under my back, my heart, anywhere where I am sore... neck, hip, eyes. I can really see and feel the difference. A total transformation!!!!! I have been working very physically at my job and my body is good and I know it is the mat!!!!!! We have been using the Shungite in the water of our parent's dog (she has a big tumor and she sleeps next to the WiFi router) since we are dog sitting for a week and have been turning off the WiFi, giving her turmeric with her food and Shungite water. The dog is transformed!!!!! My next purchase will be a Shungite pet pendant for her so she will get the protection she needs when the WiFi is on.

- Daniela 11/3/2017

I've had your Shungite Store products in place for about 3 weeks and noticed these changes. I bought the Home Kit as recommended. First, I do feel better, less stress with the nuggets and the stickers to protect from WIFI and radiation at my office and home office. It seems so peaceful everywhere now, more than before anyway, and people do not annoy me as much!

I put three nuggets taped to my water pipe and guess what - the water now comes out sparkling clean. There is no sediment on the pet dishes and all the soaps work better with less soap and less water! I need to remove those old faucet filters I was paying so much for! Also with the fridge magnet, all my organic produce stays very cold and crisp. The big test was cut lemons looking as fresh as the day I cut them six days later and the organic cucumbers were amazingly crisp and tasty even a week later, which is good because I buy a lot at once.

The water container with three nuggets in it tastes great - I was afraid to drink it at first because it came straight from the tap but then I remembered that if I let it sit overnight it will be activated with antioxidants and more beneficial. I need to get a larger water container, or more of them because I am drinking more water now faster than before!

I just ordered a Shungite bracelet and pendant as well as a magnet for my car. I also ordered a rubber mat with Shungite and crystals and it feels good in my shoes, under drinks, and under my pillow. I just sliced it using the paper cutter into the pieces I want. I put a slice on the driver's seat of my car and under my beverages.

I just was adopted by three homeless cats so in addition to my own four cats they get a Shungite nugget in their water dishes and have become a bit friskier - they like it. One of the cats tries to take the nugget out to play with it and one day, a possum came by and ate the nugget in the bowl... only the sand remained. I tape those nuggets everywhere and will order another home kit next month as I see the difference it makes. I want to share this wonderful gift from Gaia, thanks to all of you. Thanks also for the great customer service and your contribution to humanity through the Shungite Store, research and educational radio programs.

- Kathy 11/13/2017

I bought the home kit and a pendant. I had an experience with the pendant and was shocked when someone on one of your shows mentioned they had an experience exactly like mine. What happened was one day while wearing the two Shungite pendants and a bracelet someone was very aggravated with me for no good reason and, basically, what I call yelling at me. I'm a very sensitive person and as she was yelling at me I noticed my unusual ability to stay calm and that her yelling at me did not go thru me like a knife as that type of situation usually does. I could respond to her without taking it too personally.

Also, with the car magnet, my gas mileage appears to be up about 50 miles per tank which would be approximately four miles per gallon, but I'm still testing that out. I have trouble leaving home now because I'm so comfortable at home - I kinda hate to leave home these days. Thank you for your products.

- Deanna 12/17/2017

About a week ago I received the S4 stickers, 6 of them for various WiFi devices in the house. One of the devices was an old "very personal" laptop that has been with me for many years and even traveled across the ocean with me a number of times. Last year or so this "good friend of mine" started to slow down. You know, the startup process took forever, internet browsing resembled the old dial-up days. Yet I still decided to place the S4 sticker on it since I am used to using this computer. I attached the sticker on with tape on the side to the right of the touchpad. I started the computer and didn't notice any difference at the time but when I tried to open Internet Explorer, nothing happened. Then I tried to open my documents, nothing happened. I tried different files on the wall, the control panel... nothing. The cursor was there and moving but nothing would open. So I removed the sticker and everything started opening and filling the screen. Everything worked again; all previously unopened applications started. So, I decided to put the S4 sticker to the left of the touchpad. This time I was able to use the laptop with no problems.

But what is most amazing about it, is that since I put the S4 sticker on the left side, the computer runs like new. Unbelievable, but true. Email, downloads, browsing, everything works like a new computer. Thank you, guys.

Another proof of the power of Shungite: My black dog Dasha, the escape artist, is only scared of fireworks. Unfortunately, numbnuts in the neighborhood like to crack those fireworks several days before New Year's Eve. Scared Dasha attempted to jump over a six-foot fence but her leg got looped in the internet coaxial cable hanging along the fence. Somehow the wire got all twisted and tied around her leg. I discovered her about six hours later. She was able to chew her way out but the loop was still tied on her leg, cutting off all the circulation. I was able to remove it but at that moment it almost looked like she was going to lose her leg, it was so painful and swollen. I put her in the garage with three Shungite rocks in a bag under her mat, and three rocks in her drinking water. She drank a lot and slept on the mat. In the morning she looked better but still didn't want to walk. One day later she touched the ground with her injured leg and the following day Dasha was herself again, ready to chase some cats. I think Shungite greatly accelerated her recovery.

My other dog, a husky named Lobo, is another success story. After being rescued from horrible conditions by the humane society and adopted by me, he was never healthy. I blame the malnutrition in his past and the medications afterward. We had some success with him, but his chronic ear infection kept coming back again and again until recently when I had all dogs switched to Shungite water and when I made a pendant for Lobo. It's just a bigger rock from a bag of Shungite gravel wrapped in copper wire and attached to his collar but it seems to do the trick. In a matter of days, Lobo's ears started standing straight and symmetrical. He is not scratching them anymore and he is playful like a puppy.

- Libor 1/3/2018

I just started drinking Shungite water last night and I am stunned by some of the positive changes I am seeing already. I suspect that I am chronically dehydrated and don't drink enough water despite it being good quality spring water. I feel bloated when I drink water sometimes. I'm guessing that I'm not absorbing the water properly, it's possibly not getting into the cells. When I started drinking the Shungite water, I couldn't seem to get enough of it and drank about 1.5 liters in a short amount of time without feeling bloated. Could it be the fullerenes or something else (the electrical charge, etc) that is affecting the transport and absorption of the water? I also had very vivid dreams and woke up feeling more rested than usual and didn't even need my morning coffee! I'm looking forward to whatever other positive changes this powerful substance can bring! Thanks for being part of bringing this stone to the masses, the information and ongoing research!

- Gisele 1/30/2018

This is one strange experiment that is working. It's the toilet bowl. Just two or three days after scrubbing it, the ring that appears around the water's edge would start to come back. If not washed away quickly it would have to be scrubbed with a scratch pad and Comet.

Well, as I was scrubbing the darn thing recently I wondered if and how Shungite could help this problem. I live in an apartment so can't do anything about the water pipes. I am chemically sensitive so I need the water to sit for 36 hours before drinking. The water in the toilet gets flushed often BUT I'm not drinking this water, so how to do it?

I found a small mesh bag and dropped in three nuggets. I tied the top of the bag and opened the tank top. Inside the tank I found a small pipe leading from one part to another that didn't move. The nuggets would have to remain in the water and remain stationary so as not to come loose and clog the water as it was released into the bowl. I connected a plastic-coated black wire twister tie to one end of the bag of nuggets and looped the other end of the wire around the small pipe. Most of the bag hung down into the water. It looked like it was in a good position so I replaced the tank top and waited.

Every day when I go into the bathroom, I check the toilet bowl. It gets flushed often so I didn't expect too much. Hallelujah! The toilet bowl is as sparkling white as the day I scrubbed it on hands and knees! That was 2 weeks ago. Two weeks! Will miracles never cease?!

- Lorey 3/8/2018

My daughter put three Shungite nuggets into a fish tank (with just one fish in it) that has no filters or anything to clean it automatically. She normally has to clean it every other day, and by the second day, you can hardly see the fish. It is well over a week and the water is very clear and has never been changed. She said the water has never been so clear, even when first changing it. Wow!

- Marilyn 3/9/2018

I am impressed and wanted to share this with you...For some unknown reason, one that no one has figured out yet, my lights go out at any time of the day or night. The main breaker goes off. However, the kitchen range stays on.

I did not record the dates of them going out in November and December. The lights went out on January 4th at 11:30 pm, January 8th at 9:20 pm, January 28th at 8:30 pm; February 2nd at 6:00 pm, February 7th at 9:45 pm, February 10th at 8:30 pm, February 18th at 3:00 am, February 24th at 9:00 pm, February 27th at 2:30 am, and March 8th at 9:30 am.

I placed the Shungite sticker on the fuse box on March 13th. The lights have stayed on the rest of the month. My refrigerator is colder on a warmer setting.

I have the nuggets in my water bottle and stickers on my WiFi modem and cell phone. I wear my necklace for many hours each day. I am one happy Shungite camper and Shungite shopper. I am getting stronger. Life IS Grand in our Shungite Land! Thank you for your mission and labor for us.

- Dottiedee 4/2/2018

Walt Silva provided a custom solution to us for our nearby smart meter woes. Basically, this darn thing was keeping the both of us up all night, many times waking us up around the same time, approximately 4:30 am, and this went on for many early mornings. What he recommended is to attach a 24-inch by 36-inch steel piece of sheet metal to our house, in the direction of the smart meter, placing a smart sticker in the middle and using four S4 magnets in each corner. He also recommended grounding the sheet to the earth with a 4-foot long copper grounding rod attached with wire, which I did. We have noticed a significant difference in our sleep and energy in general. It is working and I have to wonder if Walt intuited this simple yet effective custom solution just for us. Perhaps this information will be useful for others to protect themselves. Thank you Shungite team!

- TF 5/10/2018

    I am a 64 year young lady living in Kansas. I clean houses for a living. I have two young grandchildren I care for at times, I have a 92-year-old mother I visit, do laundry for, and help her and I am married. I do garage sales on the side for a little extra. I am very busy and was exhausted and tired all the time.

    I received my Shungite kit around April 29th this year. The first thing I noticed was I had more energy, I had ambition, and I was motivated, thus all my work didn't seem so difficult for me.

    I am going for walks with my husband in the evenings now, walking a good distance each evening. I am sleeping better and I used to have a very hard time getting a good night's sleep. I now have an urge to get my house cleaned up, organized, and the desire to get it done, not 'oh I should get this house cleaned up' feeling anymore.

    My hips used to hurt me all the time. They made it hard for me to get comfortable enough to sleep at night.

They no longer bother me unless I really overdo it. I wear the nuggets in my pockets and I wear the small pad on my abdomen 24/7. I drink only Shungite water and I am thirsty now, so I drink more water each day. I am thankful for my Shungite.

- Kathy D. 6/5/2018

    I have a family member who I saw at my son's wedding on April 7th. We have been e-mailing back and forth several times a week since. All "poor me", "I am struggling", "two internet companies owe me several thousand dollars which has caused me great financial problems", and on and on. I realized that he has it within him to do better. However, he can't hear what I am saying. I sent him three nuggets and an S4 sticker for his cellphone which he received on Monday morning, yesterday.
    After being with Shungite for 2-3 hours, he received an email from one of the companies that owes him thousands. He sent the email to me. They are working on his complaint and they want to come up with a solution for him. The first positive thing he has received from them since he contacted them a few months back. He was excited about this and the possibility of getting the money owed him.
    This morning he wrote a beautiful positive post. He has his own business and he had a new customer this morning. He said he was professional and positive with him. He said he is tired, as many other people are, of stinking thinking and he is changing it!!! One more Shungite seed planted and growing.
    Thanks for all you have done and are doing to bring Shungite to the world.

- Dottiedee 6/5/2018

There are some of us in the world who are really into our energy fields, into the Quantum energies, and into using these energies for healing and believing they can do just that. Dee is one of these beautiful ladies. She loves Shungite and she expects Shungite to "do it" for her. She knows people who need Shungite in their lives will be led to her.

Today is Monday and last Friday night Dee had a relative call telling her of a relative that had fallen backwards off a ladder and hit his head on the camper step. Somehow he got up, leaving blood in the driveway, in the garage, and in the house on the way to the bathroom. When his wife got home at 6:00 in the evening, she was able to get him on the couch. She called the emergency room and they rushed him to the hospital. He was then flown to a larger hospital in another city. Immediately he was put in ICU. He was in a coma and wanted to talk, yet he couldn't. Dee got a phone call from her niece telling her all the things that were wrong with him.

Dee took a piece of paper and listed them. She wrote down his full name, name of the hospital, name of the city and state in the US. She wrote down that he was in ICU, however, she did not have a room number.

She then laid her cellphone, her new healing energy device on the paper. She asked Shungite to move into his room and to fill all the humidity with Shungite healing energies so when he breathed he would be taking those energies into his body. She asked for love, peace, and harmony to be in the room at all times. She asked for the bleeding to be stopped.

She asked for all the swelling in his body to go down and for his head to be healed of any trauma that was there and to put protection around him. She asked Shungite to make him well. She did all of this Sunday night at 8:30 pm. When the family arrived on Sunday evening he still wasn't talking and shortly he didn't know them at all.

On Monday morning his daughter walked through the door and he called her by name and asked, "where am I"? She explained to him the best she could what had happened and where he was. They got him up and he walked 25 steps. They gave him a washcloth in his right hand and told him to wash his face. He couldn't make his right hand work. They put it in his left hand and he washed his face.

That afternoon Dee talked to Shungite again asking Shungite to take the swelling and pressure out of his brain so he can use his right hand. And to heal any other spots in the body that need to be healed.

The doctor in the first hospital told the family, that he did not think the man would live. He said even if they did surgery, that with a concussion like this, people die.

The bleeding in the brain has stopped. The niece told Dee to keep up doing whatever it is that she is doing because it is really working for him.

For all listening to this, never underestimate the power of our thoughts and the power of our intentions and expectations. We are more powerful than we can imagine and with Shungite as our tool, we can have miracles like this one in our lives frequently.

Dee knows the power of her cellphone as she had used it on bites, poison ivy and on the places she had removed ticks from her husband that had been there for a day or two.

The biggest thing about Shungite is that we can limit it by our thoughts. Let's not limit it, let's let it expand and expand and do more and more than we ever imagined.

- Dee 6/5/2018

My Shungite friend Lea is 83 years old. She received her kit and then learned she had a tumor. She is taking treatments for her cancer in another state from where she lives. She is receiving chemo and radiation treatments to shrink the tumor so it leaves the body. She is 2 weeks into her treatments so she's about half way through them.

She only has her Shungite nuggets for her water with her. She is drinking Shungite water. She has noticed that when other people who are getting their treatments while she is getting hers all leave the room they are dragging themselves back to their hospital room. She feels good after treatment. She has not mentioned losing her hair yet either. She has two more weeks so we will see how she does. It's great that she feels good when others do not feel good from the same kind of treatment.

- Lea 6/5/2018

I bought a few pieces of Shungite and placed them into a 16oz bottle of Zephyrhills, after 2 hours I could already taste the difference. I sipped an original Zephyrhills and the one with the Shungite in it. I was so impressed!

- Andrea 6/11/19

I can't explain this in words, but every since I placed three small Shungite stones to my forehead, using very sticky black wire tape to keep them in position, and then going to bed, I have been 'transported' to places that, even as a 65-year-old man I simply cannot explain, or even begin to explain. I have had the most astonishing dreams: powerful, lucid, beyond belief in their intricacy and locality.

Last night I was in the cockpit of a craft that would make Concorde look like a World War 1 biplane. Every night it's the same, but a different dream. The dreams as so powerful they feel more real than reality itself. I am usually good with words, but I am unable to describe this to you properly. It is almost hyper-dimensional.

- Peter 9/25/2018

    I recently bought your Shungite nuggets. I'm using them in my distilled water. I can definitely feel the difference with the Shungite nuggets. My wife noticed that in our bed on my side there was something that looks like metal flakes. I know distilled water will help get rid of the metal and calcium buildup in your body, and adding the Shungite does the trick.
    I've been dealing with Type 2 Diabetes and I went to my doctor after using Shungite water for the last month and my blood levels were perfect. All I can say is I've noticed a big difference in not being tired as much on my days off after using this water.

- Robert Y. 10/29/2018

    A friend gave me a plastic pouch with Shungite powder in it. I was a bit skeptical, but I tried it out and was really impressed. Five years ago, I broke my leg - the top of the tibia shattered. After surgery, I had 3 plates and 13 screws holding my bone together. With therapy, I gradually regained full flexion of the knee, but the shin always felt weird, - kind of like if you had two packages wrapped in saran wrap and rubbed them together. I think it is due to scar tissue adhesion and/or facial torsion. I worked with a therapist who helped a lot, but I had to go back every couple of months for a "tune-up". Then I moved to a different city. After a year, the knee was beginning to ache frequently, and in addition to the adhesion feeling, the whole lower leg felt kind of "sludgy".

So when I got the Shungite powder pack, I put it over the knee for 20 minutes and then over the shin for 20 minutes, and I was amazed. The sludgy feeling went away and hasn't come back. The adhesion feeling returned in a day or two, but I have been using the pack regularly, and the adhesion feeling is getting less and staying away longer.

- Linda F. 10/30/2018

I was introduced to Shungite by a friend who gave me a Shungite pyramid (machined and polished, 4-sided base, 10 cm (4") each side, weighing 168 grams) and a pair of "harmonizing rods" – one soapstone and one Shungite (machined and polished, 1" diameter, 4" long, 600 grams). Some research on the Cosmic Reality website led me to understand that this is not the best form of Shungite for energy modulation or water purification; nevertheless, I decided to make the best use of what I had.

I've been keeping the Shungite rod in a glass jar of (already filtered) water for drinking, and I'm convinced it tastes better. I also fasten the rod to the kitchen tap when washing veggies or doing dishes, and I do not smell the chlorine anymore. But that could be wishful thinking (tasting, smelling).

But here is the real proof! I put the pyramid on top of the fridge, with the intention that it does the best it can to make the EMF from the motor biocompatible, and also to keep (or make) the food in the fridge wholesome and long-lasting. I just left it to do its thing, and didn't think about it until 4 days later, when I noticed that instead of condensation on the refrigeration plates, there is ice!

Oh, yeah, right! They said that Shungite would make the fridge more efficient, and you should keep an eye on the temperature. Oooops. The fridge thermometer reads -5 C. Rats! I've probably frozen the produce. But no! Nothing is frozen - Shungite really took on the task of keeping the food wholesome while modulating the EMF. I've turned the fridge thermostat down a notch and will monitor more closely. One Happy Camper!!

Linda F. 11/4/2018

I just had to share this!! For several days, I had a large pot of water sitting on top of the fridge with a Shungite pyramid in it. I was trying to get the "fridge magnet effect" before my fridge magnet arrives. It worked!

Today, I dumped the pot of water into the bird bath. Within a minute 5 small birds were drinking from it, and over the next 5 minutes, 30 to 40 little birds (at least 3 different kinds) came and drank. I've never seen that many, nor in so short a time. The only sad thing was I think it made them a little drunk - 3 or 4 of them crashed into the window as they took off, but no damage, they just bounced off and flew away.

- Linda F. 11/5/2018

I've been using Shungite for 4 months now and would like to share some of the ways I've used it, and the results. I am not energy sensitive (yet) so I cannot directly sense the change in WiFi fields, but I can attest to the magnets making the fridge run more efficiently, and the healing properties of even raw Shungite powder, to say nothing of the S4 stickers. I have relieved many a backache, muscle strain, toothache, and sore knee by putting a little pack of raw powder together with a S4 sticker over the area for 20 minutes, accompanied by a clear intention such as: "Energy is flowing freely and comfortably through the body, especially the {problem area}." I meditate a lot and have extended my pain-free sitting time from one hour to (on a good day) two hours by using the Shungite on my knees consistently.

For toothache, I actually hold a piece of raw Shungite in my mouth, sometimes for most of a day, and I have had two severe toothaches disappear in a couple of days. (The last one I had before I got Shungite lasted a full week before subsiding.)

I have made up a number of little packages of three small flat Shungite nuggets in folded-over packing tape, and I attach these to problem areas of my body (knees especially) with double-sided sticky tape. I wear these for several days at a time, removing them when I shower.
I have also placed several such packets on pantry shelves so that all the fresh fruits and veggies are within a few feet of Shungite.

We have three nuggets in the hot water urn (which keeps water close to boiling all day) and have noticed that the scale does not build up in the urn as it used to, though after two months I do notice a small amount of scale on the nuggets themselves.

Friends with whom I've shared Shungite report healing of a long-standing wrist injury, relief from strained backs, enhanced spiritual "processing", more stable and long-lasting results from chiropractic and acupuncture treatments ... the list goes on. It gives me great joy to share Shungite with friends and associates, the benefits are so

varied and personal!
With gratitude to the Cosmic Reality team.

- Linda F. 2/21/2019

I wear my Shungite pendant everyday. It makes wonderful things happen. Sometimes when I just think about something it appears. Truly a game changer.

- Odette P. 3/21/2019

I'm no stranger to your Shungite products & others, but the moment I received this pendant & put it on, I instantly felt like it was a game changer. I've been on a long road to healing via chiropractic work & now suddenly my chiropractor says I'm holding my adjustments much better.

- Yasmine W. 3/21/2019

The first miracle for me was that I met Gaia. The second miracle was how Gaia brought me to you. Within the last year, I have been seeking healing from an ailment somehow knowing it must be somewhere in the universe. I have had a condition for the last fifteen years that has greatly affected my life, preventing me from sleeping for more than two or three hours a night for a long, long time.
One good thing about this ailment is that it woke me up. It first led to me leaving a religion that has been the center of my life for the last 37 year. What was interesting is that I somehow knew deep down that there was a limitation in all

organized religion including the claimed "only true church" that I belonged to, but I somehow know it was time to leave it. I am completely surrounded by family and neighbors that are part of this religion so there were some parts of this that would be very difficult. But I was supposed to be connected to something greater.

In fact, I really knew this since I was nine years old. Since this experience, I somehow knew that religion never truly connected me to others like it was supposed to. I somehow knew that there was supposed to be some bigger connection that maybe even tied us together more tightly than I could comprehend. Then I learned about quantum mechanics and things finally started to make sense. I learned about telepathy, astral projection, and remote viewing one day and I was forever changed. I somehow knew this was possible. I learned about other beings surrounding us both in and out of our supposed reality. I learned about other beings visiting and being apart of this world.

Knowledge kept pouring into me from all sides. It all came together. I knew even more that I had to find a way to be even more open and had no idea how I would do this and where it would take me. But I must say that in these last few months I have been able to do that. And then one day when I was suffering greatly from my ailment, not sleeping for multiple days in a row. I was learning about Gaia and how she was alive and how she was, in fact, her own entity. I was also learning some things about grounding to her and it was hard for me to comprehend this, let alone know how to do this. In my agony. I somehow felt guided to walk out to my back yard and fall face first in the grass. I was there laying on the grass and essentially hugging Gaia. I started feeling something and started to cry. I started talking. Then I began pouring my heart out to her. I told her I was sorry if I ever mistreated her. I was sorry if I had views that may have showed that I didn't care about her. I told her I wanted to know her and then felt I should ask her if she could help me and I felt strongly that she could. I was filled with so much joy and love.

I continued my quest for what was real and true. Doing this I mostly used YouTube, It seemed to connect me to everything I needed. In fact, I knew was being led, probably by Gaia and even by those I couldn't see (I later learned it was most likely my Guides and Higher Self as well as Gaia, for sure). I just seemed to know when and what to click on YouTube.

As I continued learning exactly what I needed at the time from so many beautiful people I knew I was finally making those real connections that I knew must be out there. I was learning in such abundance about life, the universe, and this earth and the world and what was wrong with certain self-serving people who sought control of the earth (who I now know as Gaia), as well as seeking to control us. This was so sad to me. I know this is a very long story about how I found Shungite and how I was led to Cosmic Reality, but all these steps I now know were leading me to Shungite.

As I discovered this, I was quickly reminded of the day I laid on the grass, embracing the earth, crying out to Mother Earth. Well, that finally brings me to this current moment. I have since listened to most all of the Shungite Show Broadcasts. And, at last, I had some money and quickly went to the Shungite Store and made my first purchase (which included the Shungite EMF Package to protect my family, a necklace for me, and some additional S4 stickers for our kid's phones). I don't know yet if it will improve my ailment but one thing I know for sure is that I was led to you guys and particularly to Shungite. Thank you Nancy, Walt, Derek, and whomever else is involved in this great effort. I will be back to report how this goes for me.

- JPW 3/28/2019

    I put an auto magnet on my van a week ago. My tank is still on full! Usually it is about half full by now. Wow I am loving my Shungite magnets.

- Rosalind N. 5/20/2019

    I received my necklace and EMF protectors late last night. My pain has been at a level way past 15 if we were using a scale from 1-10. I woke up this morning able to move my arms without any pain!! I'm not sure which modality is working but I think it is Shungite. So wonderful!!

- Catherinne C.M. 5/22/2019

    Today I took two raw nuggets (from Cosmic Reality) and made earrings with shungite beads and copper wire. When I put them on something shifted. I am obsessed with Shungite, I just love it but I hadn't really felt it until now. It is like a field vibrating around my head. I am also wearing a pendant from Cosmic Reality that makes a threesome with the earrings. Now I never going to want to take them off.

- Anna J. 5/25/2019

    The power of intention. The rains are flooding in.

Where the water is coming into the basement...I placed 3 shungite stones. I asked that it help the water to reframe from flooding my basement. This morning the floor is DRY!

- Roslynn H. 5/28/2019

My son was showing someone a bracelet he bought in DC to reduce EMF from phones. He did the muscle test, with no phone - strong arm, with the phone - arm down, with the phone and bracelet - arm still up but much weaker. I asked him to hold my Shungite necklace while holding the phone and do the muscle test, his arm was just as strong as without the phone. INCREDIBLE!

- Marilyn 5/28/2019

Since Shungite has come into my life, I feel as though a shroud has been lifted off of me. I was quite literally addicted to social media. I never even intended to join the crowd as I've always done things on my terms and questioned everything. I first joined social media to stay connected with my sister who moved to another state and the effect trickled down to reconnecting with thousands of old friends and family around the world. I then became a stay at home mom and joined Network Marketing and Social Media was just so easy to work my businesses from my fingertips. I couldn't disconnect. I would turn off my notifications so that I would stay off my phone, but even then I would go searching for it. It actually took way more time to log back in just to see it.

My mom has been talking about Shungite for years and told me to look into it. It was one of those things that was kind of in one ear and out the other. I believed in the power it could have, but I already had stuff going on to help protect me like plants, salt rock lamps, essential oils and diffusers, CBD oil, smudging, etc. It was just another thing to add to my growing list and it was placed on hold.

I went to my mom's house a few weeks ago and she finally got her hands on some Shungite. She had me hold a Shungite pyramid and I instantly knew it was special and I had to have it. It helped me put the phone down and I have since deleted all my social media apps from my phone, actually all apps, except one that I use to video chat with my sister, and GPS. I know it's still a smartphone and it still carries harmful radiation, but this was such a huge step for me. It's amazing how different I feel and the things I'm beginning to see, hear and dream again. There's so much that is missed when you are constantly distracted.

I just started the second Cosmic Reality book and I feel the Shungite along with your enlightening research and words have been helping me get my intuition back. I can't thank you all enough<3 Now to get my loved ones back. If I have to hide a smart sticker on their phone and in their shoe, so be it!

- Julissa H. 6/5/2019

As soon as the Shungite S4 pad arrived my husband and my cat took it away from me LOL... you can feel a lot of vibration coming from the pad, and the sensation is one of immediate relief. I bet it is an anti-stressor for humans and animals. It surely revitalizes things as you place them on the pad. The round pads are also very useful for the neck area (and of course other areas such as the knees). I had a nap sleeping with the pad on my lower back and I had an interesting nap - quite a shamanic journey type of nap. The S4 pads are quite interesting - the combination of materials creates somehow something "new".

- Barbara M. 6/6/2019

My 9-day tumbled Silver Shungite is so powerful. I carry it in my pocket with two regular raw Shungite nuggets. I will purchase more of the 9-day tumbled Silver Shungite nuggets when I can. It actually makes a force field around me when someone is trying to verbally attack me or trigger me. I will NOT feel the need to respond negatively like I used to. Instead, I can process my feelings at my own pace. Then I can articulate my feelings and thoughts in a calm and dignified manner. I am so proud of myself for this balanced control of myself, something I had very little of in the past, now I am the master of my domain!! I control what thoughts I have, I no longer entertain negative thoughts or feelings. I am so appreciative and grateful to Shungite and the Shungite family. Thank you!! Thank you!!! Thank you!!!

- Annette T. 6/17/2019

I have a magnet and 2 nuggets fixed to my car seat bracket and my car runs a LOT more smoothy and I seem to get a few more km out of a tank.

- Doona H. 6/20/2019

For over 25 years I've been trying to clean up our drinking water. We've used Reverse Osmosis water for 28 years and spent hundreds on various structure devices to make it so my system can process it, rather than it just sitting in my stomach and sloshing around not being able to hydrate me. Every upgrade helped for a while. I've added minerals. You name it, I've done it. A few days ago the lightbulb came on and I decided to tape three Shungite nuggets to the outside of my glass drinking water container. Yesterday was the first time in years I've been able to drink a full half gallon of water throughout the day and feel satisfied, and not be sloshing around, which is very uncomfortable. I've been getting very dehydrated over the years simply because I have not been able to process water. I'm very pleased. Thanks Nancy and crew.

- Carolyn S. 6/21/19

I want to update any one inquiring about what magnets or stickers can do, they work in cutting energy usage in half!!!

- Linda S. 6/22/2019

I have had the pleasure of having Shungite in my life since March 2019. I am now noticing that my hair on my head is getting THICKER. I am over 40 years old and like to think that I take care of myself to the best of my ability however I am over weight. I am detecting a noticeable change in the thickness of my hair. It seems I have a whole crop of new hair growing in that is about 2 to 3 inches long right now. I feel a big difference especially when I wash my hair. Plus I looked today and noticed my wrinkles on my forehead are getting less noticeable. Shungite is simply amazing!

- Annette T. 7/4/2019

Shungite Pet Stories

Josie Dog is our longest example of the healing powers of Shungite. She was 16 years old and had that cloudy look to very old eyes. She had stopped eating and was showing labored breathing. We put a Shungite pendant on her and within days she was eating, alert, and taking walks in the back yard.

After two months of the pendant and Shungite on the electric systems and in her water, we suddenly realized her eyes no longer had that old dog look. She still had problems from her fused spine and severe arthritis, but bone takes the longest to go through any healing process. She stopped losing weight and honestly looked like a younger dog. Josie enjoyed another 2 years of living comfortably. In the end, it was not her body that gave up, as much as she needed to go on another mission.

Josie is joined by Precious Cat who had two seizures and also showed signs of healing with Shungite. After a few weeks, she had gone from a floppy cat to a cat with no noticeable problems.

And Maggy dog had been limping for over 18 months old with only very expensive surgery as the only offered solution. After a few weeks of Shungite therapy, the limp has disappeared.

One cat was not having health problems, but she sleeps with a piece of Shungite that she makes sure is where she left it.

Lanta was looking and acting her age before her owner went on a trip. Her caretaker started her on Shungite water and had put Shungite on the electric system. When they got home the owner and his partner immediately realized something was different in the house. They were also stunned to see the changes in the old and much-beloved dog. While not appearing to have been into the concept of minerals doing miracles, the changes detected due to Shungite had him order a specially created pendant of Shungite and a piece of Moldavite he had.

- NLH

In 2014, Holly my 11-year-old Jack Russell was attacked by a pack of Rottweiler cross dogs and almost killed. She had been badly mauled on her shoulders and her flanks and had to have surgery. The worst wound was on her left flank which needed to have 9 layers of stitches. The vet was amazed that she had survived such a savage attack and said that Holly would probably suffer repeated infections in the deepest wound due to bacteria from the bite. Sure enough, while the other wounds healed well, this wound would repeatedly get inflamed and start to weep fluid. Fortunately, I discovered Nancy Hopkins and Shungite. I attached a Shungite pet pendant to her collar and put three Shungite nuggets in her water. From that point on her wound never got infected again. Thank you, Cosmic Reality Shungite!

- Jan S. 11/20/2014

A childhood friend of mine that I haven't spoken to in years contacted me on Christmas Day to send his greetings. In speaking with him, he sent me a picture of his beloved four-legged 14-year-old best friend "Archie" and told me that he was not doing well. Archie wouldn't eat, drink, had no energy and was constantly shaking. He stated that Archie was also exhibiting signs of "doggie dementia". The dog couldn't focus and was just not acting like the same dog since they moved into a new home about four months ago. My intuition was telling me that this situation called for a "Shungite 911 Emergency House Call" to see what was going on. When we arrived at the house, the dog was almost unresponsive, shaking and had zero energy. The dog also did not want to be inside of the house. That was a huge sign that this dog was very sensitive to the EMF frequencies and that we needed to implement a "Shungite Environment" and see if there would be any changes. We immediately put a pendant on Archie and explained how to put the nuggets in his water bowl also. We also put an "EMF Bucky Bag" on the main wifi router in the home and also gave his owner a pendant to wear.

    Almost IMMEDIATELY after putting the pendant on the dog he snapped back into life! He started wagging his tail and allowing us to pet him. Within an hour, Archie was drinking the Shungite water and eating! His owner couldn't believe the difference (especially in his eyes) and declared this a "Shungite Christmas Miracle". Since then, he has taken Archie to the vet and he was in fact diagnosed with kidney issues. His blood will be stabilized by lots of Shungite water, special diet, and natural herbs until his kidneys can function properly again. His owner stated that nine months ago, his blood work was normal, and he believes 100% that, since moving into his new home four months ago, the dog's health declined due to his sensitivity to the wifi systems in his home. He is beyond grateful for Shungite and believes that every house needs a Shungite environment. He said it was amazing to feel this way because we have been living so long surrounded in EMF pollution that we don't even know what it feels like to feel normal and balanced again".

- Stephanie 4/30/2015

I've waited three weeks to write to you. My old chicken, Sophie, (5 yrs old) was at death's door three weeks ago. I had such a heavy heart thinking I was going to lose her. (I know I must sound crazy to you because I love each and every one of my 15 chickens) Anyway, I had a thought, why not put Shungite in her water!? So I did. She drank a small amount and just laid there. As the day went on she drank more and by the end of the day, she ate a very little of her feed. She was very weak for about two days but I could see a little improvement each day.

Now, three weeks later she is running around the yard with her sisters. From the bottom of my heart Nancy I thank you for bringing Shungite into my life.

- Dottie 6/10/2016

I have a little Bichon, a 10-year-old doggie. For the last 4-5 years, she has had red yeast on her back from the base of her tail up 2/3's of the way towards her head. At the base, it was 2 inches wide and in a V shape towards the head. I used several different natural remedies, and nothing ended it for her. She has been on the Shungite water for 2 months now and has worn a pendant for 5 weeks and she is now snow white on her back. She is so beautiful.

Also, she was peeing all over the floors throughout the house. That is what old dogs do, so I was told. Well, she is now using her potty papers as that is what puppies do!! She is younger! She is my Shungite puppy dog now!! So lovable and she wants to be with me rather than just laying around on the couch. She wants up on my lap more and is a happier puppy. She loves to go outdoors now and will stay out by herself. She is my Shungite happy puppy. Of course, my whole house is a Shungite home. Shungite is amazing. All pets can benefit from being in a Shungite home. Thank you all at Cosmic Reality Shungite for giving my puppy a new young life.

- Dottiedee 5/14/2018

    GeeDee is my 15-year-old Belgian Shepherd/ Brittany Spaniel mix dog. She was the runt of the litter and did not get all of the nutrition that she needed as a newborn and young puppy. She has always had difficulty with her hind legs but especially so now that she has a rather large tumor on her left hip. She has been a typically acting old dog for the last couple of years, that is until April. In April we were introduced to Shungite by Dottiedee. GeeDee has Shungite nuggets in her water and she wears a Shungite key ring on her collar. Since having Shungite available to her she has been acting and playing like the puppy she was many years ago. She bounds into the house and plays with the 2-year-old Labrador Retriever who lives with her and she is seemingly a much younger dog than her 15 years. I marvel at the miracle of Shungite and my young old dog. Thank you, Nancy, and Dottiedee for sharing Shungite with us. I am thankful every day.

- Suzy 6/8/2018

    We have a 16-year-old poodle rescue named Indie. She has kidney disease and had a very bad experience due to her kidneys shutting down recently. She was so weak that she couldn't even stand up and was vomiting everything she ate or drank. She was hospitalized for the weekend and her strength returned but the vet said her blood work indicated that she was in Stage Four of Renal Disease. He told us that "this is the beginning of the end" and tried to prepare us for her soon to come death. We initiated Shungite water and gave her a Shungite pendant. I lined her two sleeping beds with Jade (a specific for kidney disease) and lots of Shungite. She is much stronger now, eats, and is her loving and affectionate self again. A bonus is that she was trembling all the time, for months, and the trembling has ceased completely!

She is still an aged poodle and sleeps a lot but when she is awake she still likes to play with her ball and the other dogs. She gets up in the morning and absolutely RUNS to her toys and then is excited to go outside. She is a new dog! The last time we had her groomed the groomer (who works with our vet) commented that she was once covered with warts and that it was hard to groom her because the warts were everywhere. She asked us what we were using because all the warts were gone or drying up! We explained about our Shungite treatments and promised to bring her a pendant the next time we brought the dogs in for grooming. We are so happy with Shungite and now all the dogs (we have 3 of them) are wearing pendants and drinking Shungite water. I am ecstatic to note that I only need 3 Shungite nuggets to cleanse a large container of water and that I no longer need to cleanse and charge them as I do my other crystals. What a discovery! Thanks for all you do to get the news of Shungite out to everyone!

- Sherry R. 7/15/2018

Shungite water everyday is making the hair grow back around my dog Shin's right eye!

- Anita S. 5/24/2019

My cat has an S4 pendant and his fur looks much more shiny and healthy. He also feels more relaxed...he is already pretty relaxed but now he looks as if he is in the Caribbean drinking a non-alcoholic Margarita!!!

The dog felt left out of the band, but he has got a pendant too now and seems happy as Larry. They are drinking more water since we put 3 nuggets in their drinking bowl and we jumped over the fence to put some Shungite on our neighbor's well from where we get our water.

- Barbara M. 6/6/2019

Update on my dog Diesel. In just three days he is feeling and doing so much better!! His hot spots are going away!! His mood is elevated!! He is all smiles besides running and jumping around!! Both of his hot spots are drying up and healing and the other two hot spots that were coming out are now gone!! I did what Nancy Hopkins suggested; I rubbed my S4 sticker on his hot spots and pictured the excess energy flowing out of him down into the earth, gave him Shungite charged water, and he is in a Shungite environment. And now as Derek Condit suggests I will be giving him 1/4 teaspoon of Shungite honey twice a day and rubbing a bit of the honey on the hots pots to help heal them. Such a beautiful demonstration of what people can do when they focus their good energy.

- Annette T. 6/8/2019

Derek, Maureen, Nancy, and Walt:

I got my bee nugget order shortly after my butterfly bush flowered back in April, May. I placed three nuggets at the base of the tree. The flowers dropped off too soon, sooner than my neighbors so I was very disappointed, the bush wasn't looking good. That bush flowers in spring, by the way, I am in zone 4a.

Here it is August when I went outside and I spotted new blooms on the butterfly bush, second blooming and completely out of season for it to be flowering here in the Colorado mountains!!! Can you believe it?

That is one thing. Another thing was that I have a water softener. I had three elite nuggets that someone gave me and I threw one nugget into the tank.

I also have a water distiller since our CO water is super hard and full of heavy metals. It had been about one year since I cleaned my distiller and I was afraid to open it because I should have cleaned it every three months. My nugget had been in the water softener for 3 weeks then I dropped two more in the tank two days ago. This distiller runs for hours every day. I bought it back in 1985, it's 34 years old.

When I opened my distiller, I found all the hardness had crumbled into sand size pieces at the bottom of my distiller. All I had to do is to wipe up all the sand and it is completely clean. You have no idea how hard it is for me to clean that distiller because it can get so thick in there after three months and I had neglected it for an entire year!!! When I clean it, I have to use this nasty chemical powder which takes two weeks to break up all the hardness and that means we have to buy water for those two weeks.

I was excited beyond belief because it was so easy and now I am looking at not having to ever clean it the old way again!

One thing Walt said is that sometimes equipment that is not in very good shape or old, might be accelerated to its demise. Well, my house is 23 years old and the hot water tank started leaking rust from the underside. Furthermore, my hot water dispenser gave up the ghost at the same time as all this happening with my distiller..

I just checked on my water tank and the leaking has become clean which means the shungite cleaned all the hard water at the bottom of the tank. Interesting? Some plumbing may have to be done here...

I had purchased powder which disappeared from the package you guys sent me then I bought some more and I told it not to go away. I proceeded to buy paint and put the powder in it.

I painted a transformer which is in front of our house. I also painted the gas meter, the electric meter, the water meter, and the circuit breaker boxes. I don't have numbers for you as to the savings on the bills yet.
I also painted small patches on the under side of every computer in the house and cell phones.

I thought you guys would like to know what all shungite is doing here in Colorado mountains.

Your good customer,

Carmen

Dear Maureen,

I made my shungite hummingbird feeders, they love it, there are only a few of them but they are standing right at the shungite I glued on the rim of the feeder.
Remember I told you I had ordered powder and it was on my desk, still in the package and it disappeared?
Well, now I got someone else's shungite phone protector, where did it come from? Who lost it? It's here on my desk. I guess it was an exchange.

I looked all over the website and I don't see the phone protector at all, it's not from your website. The ones you have don't look like this one. It is rectangular with gold on the back, it is shungite for sure, I just checked it.

I looked at my receipt just in case I am losing my mind but I have not ordered this item. What is going on? I am new to shungite, you and Derek have been doing this for a while, what is this?

Why do these stones come and go? I don't understand......

-Carmen

Dear Nancy and all: Listened to Shungite Radio when you talk about putting Shungite nuggets on water pipes. Well I put one Oraphim shungite sticker on my cold water pipe and like you said no chlorine smell and softer water and better suds in the water when washing pots etc, my neighbors are witnessing the same reaction on not having it on their pipes: so, I have covered 6 flats or whatever and I am well impressed with other household electrical items like you explain that there is a 20 % + in electrical reduction etc ...... Question: If the Shungite spins the atoms at whatever incredible revolutions 'P-S ', in the clockwise rotation in water which is proven! Then can the same principle apply to gas in the gas pips would it improve the gas molecular structure as similar to what it does to water? Gods speed

- Magan Tyson

Ok. I'm going to be honest and tell you I was skeptical. But I spent a chunk of money w the hope yal are on to something w shungite. Enough for my four colonies. First year Beek here. I've done a ton of research. And had a very very weak hive. Put shungite powder and rocks in the entrance and let them be. Less than a month later and we are seeing a significant increase in resources coming in. More than my bigger hives. Significantly more. Thank you for what you're doing. Me and my bees thank you.

- Facebook post

Last night my grandson, 8, was tearing up over his mouth inside and out hurting due to his braces. It was all raw and looked painful. We dropped some caster oil on it and it still hurt so I gave him the free pouch of shungite powder purchased from your store. He put it on his mouth and went to sleep. This morning he said the oil didn't work but the shungite did. "Why?" he asked. I said "I don't know, it's healing." As Catholics, when I gave him the shungite powder pouch last night I told him it's from outer space and is a healing stone and God made everything that's good. He said "God made us." He had no complaints of his mouth hurting this morning. I also put a shungite car magnet on the metal part by the seat. No one knows it's there. But I take comfort in it protecting them during the 5 hour trip home. Thank you!

- Diane M 12/29/19

Chapter 3

Frequently Asked Questions

1. Q: What is Shungite?

A: There is only one Shungite source in the world. It is the Zazhoginsky Shungite deposits in the western Republic of Karelia, near the eastern border of Finland. The word "Shungite" is derived from the small town in the area called Shunga. While some would disagree, we believe the Shungite deposit resulted from a meteorite strike 2.5 billion years ago. What remains is 1000 square km (386 square miles) of a mix of materials having very unique qualities and attributes.

Composition of Elite Shungite
National Science Center,
Institute of Physics and Technology

Element	Min	Max
C	83,4	89
O	10,3	15,8
Si	<0,1	0,1
S	0,3	0,5
Cl	0,1	0,2
K	0	<0,1
V	<0,1	<0,1
Ni	0	<0,1
Na	0	
Ca	0	<0,1

Composition Raw Shungite

Element	Min	Max
C	49,1	54,7
O	27,3	31,6
Na	0,1	0,2
Mg	0,2	0,2
Al	0,9	1,1
Si	14,8	16,7
S	0,2	0,3
K	0,6	0,7
Ca	0,1	0,2
Ti	0	0,3
Fe	0,3	0,6

Carbon - C Silicon - Si Chlorine - Cl Vanadium - V Sodium - Na Iron - Fe Aluminum - Al
Oxygen - O Sulfur - S Potassium - K Nickel - Ni Calcium - Ca Magnesium - Mg Titanium - Ti

In a study done by the National Science Center Kharkov Institute of Physics and Technology (NSC KIPT), eleven significant elements were identified as being found in both Elite and Raw Shungite, although the elements differed between the two types of Shungite.

The chart above lists the elements contained in the two types of Shungite normally encountered by users of Shungite. A third type is used mainly for industrial and construction purposes and has an even lower amount of carbon, and is more grey than black.

Elite (also referred to as Noble) Shungite has a much higher carbon content than what we call "Raw Shungite". Pure Elite is shiny and brittle. Raw looks like coal and the darker the black the higher the carbon content.

The above chart shows the other elements contained in the two types of Shungite. They differ in the amount of each element and the elements of magnesium, aluminum, titanium and iron are present in Raw but not in Elite Shungite. Trace amounts of vanadium and chlorine are only found in Elite Shungite.

Everyone, including myself, attributes the seeming magic of Shungite to be associated with a carbon molecule called a C60. The more carbon, the more C60 molecules. Thus, Elite will have many more C60 molecules than the Raw Shungite. However, there is much more at play than the number of C60 molecules.

Why does Elite Shungite even exist? If we think of a stew, reportedly containing every element in the Periodic Table of Elements, suddenly heating up to as much as 3,000 degrees F (1,650 degrees C) as it fell to Earth, we would see it begin to change. Chemistry and the attraction of certain elements to each other would cause a type of clumping from the heating and "stirring". That is why Elite is very different when looking at the other trace elements it contains.

What actually happened is this composite mineral ball traveling through Interstellar Space entered Earth's atmosphere. The friction, as the ball fell through the atmosphere, caused the ball to become a burning meteorite on a huge scale. Even after hitting Earth, this near molten deposit continued "cooking". When it cooled, veins of Elite Shungite were contained within the deposit of the Raw Shungite. Extracting pure Elite from the massive Shungite deposit is difficult and expensive.

Elite and Raw Shungite are very different chemically and energetically. We believe that while many may resonate with Elite, the qualities of Raw are a better match for the 3D physical environment. We do not sell Elite and everything discussed in this book is based upon Raw Shungite.

2. Q: *If Elite does not have any iron, why do I see rust on my Elite nuggets?*

A: Elite Shungite is formed as veins within the Shungite deposit. Some Elite specimens are pure while others at the edge of the vein may also contain some of the elements contained in Raw shungite. This contamination of the pure Elite vein by iron will sometimes show up in the Elite specimen as rust when the iron is exposed to water. The rust is not dangerous.

3. Q: *Why do I see rust on my Raw nuggets along with silver/gold streaks?*

A: In the chart of elements, Raw Shungite has iron (Fe) and sulfur (S). When mixed together you can get pyrite as streaks or as actual cube-like crystals. Iron subjected to water can result in rust that is not dangerous.

4. Q: *Is Pyrite toxic?*

A: A combination of Iron and Sulfur, Pyrite has a bad reputation for being a major toxic problem, but only in mining operations. It is the Sulfur that is toxic, which can be released from the Pyrite matrix during mining, creating sulfur dioxide gas when exposed to water. Assuming the Pyrite releases sulfur into your drinking water that becomes sulfur dioxide gas in very trace amounts, there is not enough gas to be of any danger. On top of that, all toxins in water are transmuted by Shungite. If sulfur dioxide was a problem, it would certainly have been detected as an environmental hazard. What we find instead is pristine water in the lakes in and surrounding the Mother Lode in Karelia.

Do not worry about pyrite. You cannot possibly get as much sulfur dioxide in your water as you find in some processed food. From the Agency for Toxic Substances & Disease Registry: *"Ingestion of sulfur dioxide is unlikely because it is a gas at room temperature. Sulfur dioxide is used in small amounts as a food and wine preservative. Highly sensitive asthmatic individuals can develop bronchospasm after eating foods or drinking wine preserved with sulfur dioxide or other sulfur preservatives."*

Shungite.Com states:

"Shungite has the ability to clean water from almost of all organic compounds (including pesticides), metals, bacteria and harmful microorganisms.

The water from Lake Onega in Russia, can be used for drinking without any prior cleaning! It's the result of thousands of years of interaction with Shungite. The commercial use of Shungite filters started back in 1990's, during that time, many experiments and studies were conducted on Shungite influencing health on the human body. Scientists came to the conclusion that Shungite water is absolutely non-toxic.

Quartzite and pyrite are natural components of classical shungite. They are unevenly distributed in the stone and are well visible. While treating shungite water and other uses of shungite – the content and quantity of these insertions does not have matter."

5. Q: *What is Shungite good for?*

A: When first meeting up with Shungite in March 2014 the following list answered the question. It still applies and we will discuss the various categories of Shungite's attributes in the following sections.

Shungite Is Used For:

- water purification and infusion of water with healing energies;

- enhancement of growth in vegetation and livestock;

- EMF, microwave, and nuclear shielding materials;

- healing a variety of diseases;

- creation of healing rooms by Russian Military Medical

clinics;

- balancing the energy body that is the blueprint for the physical body, promoting physical, emotional, and mental health;

- charging bath water and swimming pools;

- a Shungite pendant provides balance and individual protection against most types of EMF & microwave fields.

6. Q: *Are people reporting health enhancements with Shungite?*

A: If you have read the testimonials in the previous chapter, you know that some amazing health enhancements are being reported, as they have been reported for at least 300 years.

To be considered relevant by the establishment, research has to be "Peer Reviewed". This designation of a research report indicates it has been reviewed by one's "peers", in other words, as one's "equals". A group of people NOT affiliated with any government/corporate/academic agenda, that would be us average, uncertified people who share our observations, is a much better pool of accurate and honest reporting.

That being said, there have been continual certified health benefits recorded by certified organizations and individuals throughout the world regarding the health benefits of Shungite.

7. Q: *How do you determine you have real Shungite?*

A: This test is for nuggets and figurines. Beads, Shungite Resin products and Shungite Powder do NOT pass the test because conductivity is lost.

1. Take any typical, cheap flashlight and turn it on.
2. Unscrew the cap which has a spring in it.
3. DO NOT remove the battery compartment.
4. Place the nugget or figurine so it touches the center metal piece in the battery holder while the other end touches the spring in the cap.
5. If the flashlight lights up, it is Shungite.

Beads can sometimes be tested this way, if you can maintain pressure so each bead touches the others. But streaks of gold, silver or white indicates it is real Shungite. Not all the beads will have the streaks but if none of them do, it may not be genuine. Also the inside of the hole in the beads should be black not white.

8. Q: What is Enerology?

A: Enerology is the study of Energy.

My introduction to Metaphysics came during the late 1980s. The word Metaphysics comes from Ancient Greece, where it was a combination of two words – Meta, meaning over and beyond – and physics. Metaphysicians fundamentally believe that what we consider as being real and provable by traditional physics is only a manifestation from an energy universe. "Real" is what our physical senses perceive and what we construct in our consciousness as something tangible. But even Albert Einstein came to realize:

> "Concerning matter, we have been all wrong. What we have called matter is energy, whose vibration has been so lowered as to be perceptible to the senses. There is no matter."

While having no certificate proving I am a scientist that will satisfy those who need such certification for validation, a scientist is simply someone who systematically gathers and uses research and evidence, develops a hypothesis and tests it, to gain and share understanding and knowledge. I am a scientist.

By the time my path took me into the world of Metaphysics, I had traveled through the world of Electronic Warfare where the battlefield was one of invisible electromagnetic signals from radio to radars. That energetic world introduced me to Quantum Physics where it was looking like all that is, is energy. We live in an energy universe. To quote Einstein again: *"Matter is Energy ... Energy is Light ... We are all Light Beings."*

Biology is the study of biological life. Enerology is the study of energy. Enerology was a term I began using when discussing what I was seeing as a merging of Quantum Physics and Metaphysics. Quantum Physics was devising ways of testing, measuring, analyzing, and comprehending the Energy Universe. Metaphysicians had been developing a knowledge base of how to harness the Energy Universe. Metaphysicians have been considered quacks by accepted scientific establishments because their theories and successes entered into the realm of magic. And indeed that is true. But magic is just the manipulation of energy.

Metaphysicians are magicians harnessing the magic accessed by an understanding of the Energy Universe.

Enerology studies the claims of Metaphysicians within the context of what is known in Quantum Physics. It also delves into new avenues of cosmic energy by following the claims of energy healings, shamanic travels, divination, telepathy, astral projection, angels, spirits, souls and so forth.

Energy cannot be created or destroyed, it can only be changed from one form to another. Shungite showed us toxins can be eliminated from water, soil and air. Detoxification of water has been known for at least the last 300 years, while soil and air detoxification are recent discoveries. These claims are proven facts. But how does Shungite do it, was the perplexing question never answered until energy intuitive individuals got into the picture. Such people fall into the category of metaphysicians. The metaphysicians could see the field of Shungite connected to the Quantum Field through the molecule C60 rotating at over 20 billion times per second. The resulting energy field overpowers toxic molecules rotating in a way that is harmful to the health of all living things. A toxic molecule loses molecular cohesion, breaking apart into the individual atoms comprising it.

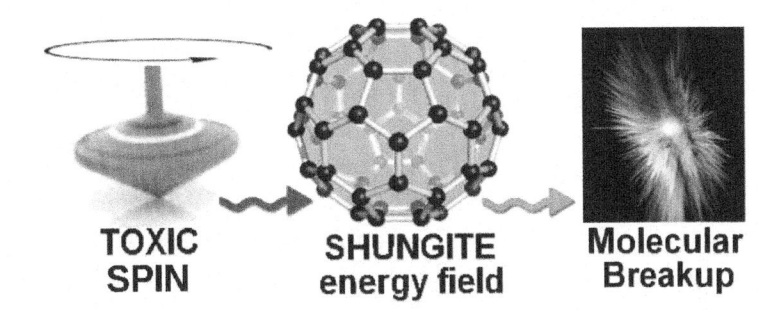

TOXIC SPIN → **SHUNGITE energy field** → **Molecular Breakup**

EM/WiFi/Radiation fields being energy only, simply undergo a reversal of rotation without loss of signal strength.

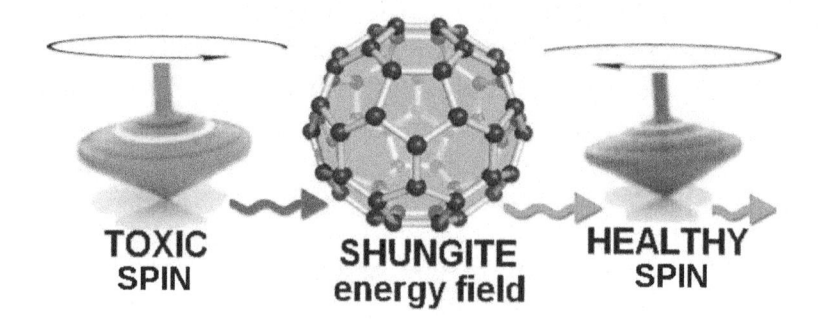

TOXIC SPIN   **SHUNGITE energy field**   **HEALTHY SPIN**

9. Q: Do you have to clean and recharge Shungite?

A: Except for an initial washing to remove Shungite powder and anything else that might be on the nuggets, neither cleaning nor charging is ever required. Shungite's surface accumulates dust during processing and shipping. We recommend keeping the water used to clean off the dust to put on plants. Why clean something that cleans water, soil, and air? Shungite is, after all, linked to the Quantum Field and there is nothing more powerful than that, which is why it also does not require recharging.

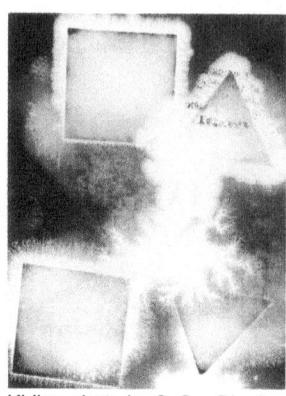

Kirlian photo by Sofiya Blank

10. Q: Why are three nuggets recommended to energize water?

A. From the beginning, we were aware that each nugget and, in fact, each particle of powder, has a unique signature beyond the base Shungite energy. When any three pieces or particles get within range of each other, their fields create a secondary field that is "coherent" or has added stability. The Kirlian photograph of geometric shaped Shungite pieces demonstrates that secondary field. You can see the individual fields and an additional field linking three pieces of Shungite together.

11. Q: What is a Shungite grid and how do I make one?

A: A "grid" is a term used in energy work to indicate different sources of energy being brought together for some specific purpose. Most known is a pattern made up of different crystals and minerals. In a Shungite grid, Shungite is being used. When applied to the "Shungite World Grid", it indicates Shungite is being placed all over the world and the "grid board" is Earth itself. Individuals have been placing Shungite anywhere they get the urge to do so. To find out more search "Cosmic Reality Shungite World Grid."

DRINKING WATER

12. Q. What is the difference between "Shungite Water" and "Shungite Energized Water"?

A: Using three Raw Shungite nuggets, either wrapped on a pipe or in a drinking container, creates "Shungite Energized Water". "Shungite Water" is created using a pile of nuggets; takes 48 hours to activate; needs recharging monthly; and has to be replaced every six months. The difference is one of perception. We look at a universe comprised of energy. Others see a materialistic and chemical universe.

13. Q: What is "Shungite Energized Water"?

A: Shungite Energized Water has its water molecules excited by a Shungite Energy Field. The water molecules instantaneously begin spinning and become "alive" energetically.

Water flowing freely in nature has a spin at the molecular level. You can clearly see water moving and churning while in the stream. When you take a sample out of the stream, at the molecular level there is still movement. The water is essentially alive even outside the stream. But sooner or later the water will lose the molecular spin and at the energetic level the water becomes lifeless.

When this lifeless water is in a pipe connected to your house and it encounters a Shungite energy field, the water molecules entering the field begin spinning and become alive. Every water molecule in the Shungite field begins spinning and the field can go out a number of feet depending upon the carbon content in the Shungite.

In actuality, the Shungite energy field does not have to be very large. The Shungite field is connected to the Quantum Field where proto-energy continually fuels the powerful spin of the Shungite field. Molecules of water begin spinning and influence the surrounding molecules through the concept of resonance. Energy fields with similar frequencies begin to vibrate in unison. If you strike the middle C on a piano, all the other C notes begin to play but do not affect the music. The strings are not vibrating loud enough to be heard, but they can be seen "resonating" with the note that was struck.

The first water molecules entering the Shungite field begin spinning. The resonance frequency causes any other water molecule in close proximity to also begin spinning. This continues layer by layer back up the pipe or down the pipe until encountering a valve. You do not have to have a Shungite field where all the water is within it. Sympathetic Resonance begins with water molecules inside the field; but resonance expands the energetic reaction beyond the Shungite field.

Shungite spinning, energized water has a tendency to feel softer. Softer water has fewer minerals that form calcium or magnesium salts which leave a "soap" film in the shower or bath tub. Hair also has a more desirable cleansing in soft water because there are fewer of the insoluble deposits left on the hair. Using a Shungite water supply results in far less or no deposit build-ups, as testified by our customers.

The indication of softer water and therefore of fewer minerals in the water is another sign of Shungite's ability to detoxify water. The Shungite energy field is so extremely powerful that any toxic energy field from a molecule dangerous to life begins to reverse. This reversal of the spin of the energy field of the toxic molecule causes the molecule to lose its cohesion and break down into harmless atoms.

14. Q: How many Shungite nuggets should I use to "energize" my drinking water?

A: Three Raw nuggets placed in a container of drinking water is all you will need. To energize your home's water system, put three small to medium-sized nuggets on the **cold** water intake to your water heater using tape to hold the nuggets to the pipe. The nuggets do not have to touch each other, but they do need to be near each other. Normally the cold water and hot water pipes at the heater are close enough that the nuggets will energize both pipes. We recommend the cold pipe for the nuggets as the hot water pipe will cause the tape to deteriorate.

15. Q: Why do you recommend nuggets in the toilet tank?

A: The resonance effect is lost when a valve interrupts the physical connection of the water molecules. When the valve in your toilet tank stops the flow of water and the connection to the energized water molecules, the water in the tank will eventually lose its spin. We recommend putting three nuggets in the water tank in a corner of the tank.

16. Q: Is it better to use Raw Shungite or Elite Shungite to energize my drinking water?

A: We recommend using Raw Shungite large enough to avoid them being swallowed accidentally. Elite Shungite is not necessary, nor is it necessary to use any more than three nuggets. If you use a glass container, make sure it is strong enough to withstand the nuggets bumping around as the container is used.

17. Q: Is it OK to use the Shungite nuggets in water in a plastic container? Other websites advise against, but I see no mention one way or the other on yours.

A: My read on Shungite is that even in a plastic container leaching chemicals, which I would never use without Shungite, Shungite can transmute those toxins. My personal feeling is using Shungite in plastic is fine when it is the best option for travel (do NOT allow the plastic to heat up in a hot car). However, others would say do not take a chance and never use plastic. Glass is the recommended container. Many glass containers now have silicon covers that will help in case of accidental glass breakage but you can also purchase them separately; search for "silicon glass covers". There is evidence that metal containers can potentially flake off small particles that should not be ingested.

18. Q: Does the PH change in Shungite Energized Water?

A: This seems to be an "urban legend". It appears to come from a Shungite Water Purifier company that makes the claim, which has gone on to be widely shared. The manufacturer wanted to sell another addition to their product that would keep the PH alkaline. Numerous tests of the PH, with from three to a handful of nuggets and with Shungite powder in the water, have NEVER seen the PH change one way or the other.

19. Q: Do you have to clean and recharge Shungite?

A: Neither cleaning nor charging is ever required of Shungite. What will recharge that is more powerful than the Quantum Field that fuels Shungite? And what would you use to clean something that itself cleans water, soil, and air?

20. Q: Can Shungite energize an entire water system in a home?

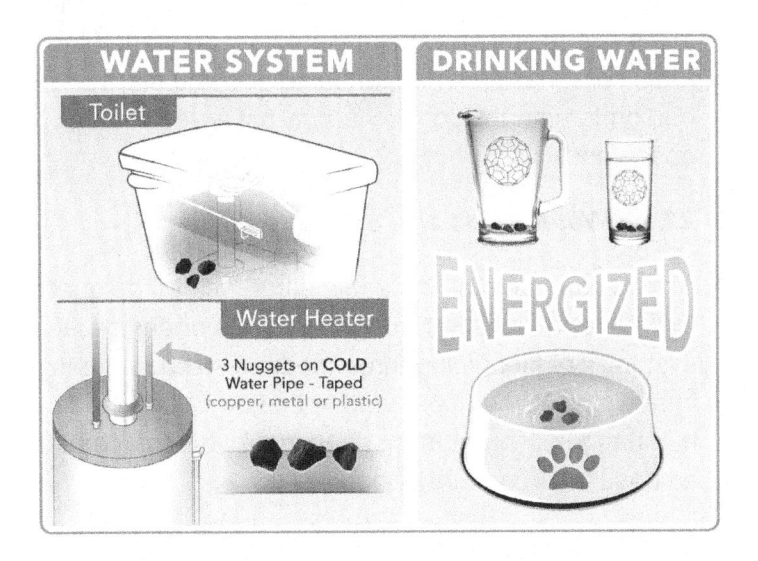

A: Yes. Three Shungite nuggets taped next to each other on a water pipe will energize all the water in the pipe. This solution is really only recommended for the cold water pipe because the tape will deteriorate on the hot water pipe. Any time water flow encounters a valve that is closed, the water on the other side of the valve will not be Shungite energized. Each toilet should have three medium-sized Shungite nuggets in the tank to keep the toilet bowl clean. There is also a valve on the hot water tank. When the cold water fills the tank a valve shuts the tank off from the cold water. Thus, the water in the tank is no longer Shungite energized water. To rectify this and to keep your water heater running more efficiently we recommend a Shungite S4 magnet be placed on the hot water tank itself.

21. Q: Why are the Shungite nuggets in my aloe vera drink shrinking?

A. Shungite nuggets will gradually "disappear" in water or Aloe Vera, as the surfaces of the nuggets are worn away. It takes a long time in water. There may be something in the Aloe Vera making it happen faster, as you are the second person to note this, or perhaps you were just more observant.

22. Q: Water Wells and Shungite

A: You can make a noticeable difference to the quality of well water by adding Shungite nuggets or devices to the system. Try just taping three medium-sized nuggets to the intake pipe to the house and notice any changes. If you see no changes or want more of an improvement, contact us for a consultation on further options.

23. Q: Swimming Pools and Shungite

A: We simply do not have enough reports to adequately

answer this question. If I had a pool, I would put three larger nuggets in the bucket that catches debris. Shungite nuggets will be worn down in flowing water, so keep an eye on them.

Shungite Water Turtle

We do have an energy device based on Shungite that Dolly Howard has in her pool. Dolly has enjoyed her energized pool for a couple of years. And this is a testimonial by one of her pool technicians.

Alex Navarro - "Shungite seem to be doing an amazing job relating to the over all well being of the pool quality."

Dolly Howard - "The above is written and attested to by my pool cleaner on 4/3/18. He is always impressed that the chemical balance is perfect. I asked him for a testimonial and he happily agreed to write the above - his words."

The Water Turtle is an energy device. It radiates a frequency tuned to the frequency of pure water. It was designed by Walt Silva after we discovered a similar "radionics device" was used to clear lakes in Europe.

24. Q: Shungite in the Garden.

A: There are numerous reports of Shungite doing amazing things with plants. You can scatter nuggets around (in groups of three nuggets). Putting nuggets in a water sprayer used to spread fertilizer has also been reported as beneficial. Another option is to put a teaspoon of Shungite powder in the water sprayer. Using the powder spreads the Shungite around and each particle of powder has its own powerful field. When using the nuggets in the sprayer, you are adding energy that will eventually dissipate. The powder being spread has a longer residual effect, until the powder breaks down into individual atoms from "wear". Repeat the spraying whenever you remember.

25. Q: What impurities are removed from water by Shungite?

A: Theoretically, Shungite transmutes molecules of toxins, radiation isotopes, and anything toxic to life with an energy field rotation contrary to what is a natural life-supporting spin. The following list is a basic one.

Shungite purifies water by removing:

- ✓ Iron
- ✓ Manganese
- ✓ Phenol
- ✓ Chlorine
- ✓ Nitrates and nitrites

✓ Free radicals
✓ Bacteria and microorganisms
✓ Bad odors
✓ Color
✓ Turbidity

Source: https://shungit-store.com/

26. Q: Why did my glass drinking container break when I put the nuggets in?

A: The glass was not strong enough to withstand clunking nuggets. If you are concerned about the nuggets breaking the glass, just put the three nuggets up against the outside of the glass. Alternative ways of energizing water are to use the Shungite S4 laminated sticker as a coaster or we also offer Shungite coasters. The water will be energized the same as if you had put nuggets of Shungite in the water.

27. Q: Why three nuggets in a drinking container?

A: Three nuggets of Shungite in any size drinking container, including pet drinking bowls, creates a "coherent" field that is more stable and energetic. The coherent field created by three nuggets is capable of creating Shungite Energized Water in any size drinking container. When any three nuggets or particles get within range of each other their fields create a secondary field that is "coherent" or has added stability.

28. Q: Why do you stress the use of three nuggets and also say size does not matter?

A: This is based upon a combination of quantum science and observations by energy sensitive people. It boils down to the three nuggets creating a "coherent" energy field. Think of it as just being more stable. The size of the individual nuggets does not matter. The critical decision regarding size depends on what you are using it for and what size works best for the application.

29. Q: Does Shungite Energized Water lose its charge?

A: Yes, but only when disconnected from the Shungite Nuggets. If you have a big container of water and nuggets and then pour the water into a small personal water container without Shungite, the water will lose its spin. For the same reason we advise putting nuggets in pet water bowls.

We proved this when we realized that the toilet tank was being disconnected from the Shungite Field every time the valve turned off the water. The valve was separating the tank water from the Shungite-charged water supply. Without the charged water in my tank, a brown goo had formed inside the tank. I also had to clean my toilet bowl a minimum of once a week. After adding three nuggets to the tank, I hardly ever need to brush the bowl because the tank does not have the brown goo.

30. Q: Why is the greasy film that used to end up on the dog bowl no longer there since adding Shungite?

A: You are talking about "biofilm". Biofilm is the result of microorganisms that can be bacteria, fungi or protists growing on the side of the bowl. One other example of biofilm is dental plaque. It is not hard to imagine how dental plaque bacteria in the pet's mouth feeds the biofilm in the bowl. This is one of the examples that show Shungite is working. Toxic microorganisms that should not be in the water are simply destroyed in a Shungite environment and no biofilm, which is the greasy covering on the bowl, is created.

31. Q: Why do I have mold growing in Shungite Energized Water?

A: This question came up twice. Without being able to conduct tests, my only answer is that the mold is not toxic. The term "toxic mold" is not accurate. While certain molds are toxigenic, meaning they can produce toxins (specifically mycotoxins), the molds themselves are not toxic, or poisonous. One complaint was of mold in Shungite sweet tea and the other was of mold in cracks at the bottom of a porcelain container.

32. Q: Why do I have rust on my nuggets?

A: The National Science Center Kharkov Institute of Physics and Technology (NSC KIPT) determined the composition of both Elite and Raw Shungite. Eleven different elements were listed as significant. In both types of Shungite, carbon is the most plentiful. While the Elite list does not include iron as part of its composition, the Raw Shungite lists iron in the 11th place. It is the iron that turns to rust but it is not dangerous.

33. Q: Is it true that metals in Shungite can leach into my water?

A: If this was true, Shungite would be poisonous. Instead, the water in the Shungite Mother Lode can be used for drinking without any prior cleaning! Furthermore, they use Shungite in water purification systems without any build-up of toxins. While we have not directly tested Shungite Energized/Shungite Water, it is likely that the various university-sponsored research into Shungite have. There are no credible sources to suggest that this is cause for concern.

SHUNGITE AND ELECTRO-MAGNETIC RADIATION

34. Q. Is there any proof your stickers actually work?

A: It depends on what you consider "proof". Since May 2014 we have had thousands of customers compared to less than a dozen requests for a refund. We have a 100% guarantee, no questions asked return policy.

When we finally found someone who could use thermography to look at a cell phone with and without the Shungite S4 sticker, we saw the first measurable effects. Thermography reads heat. A transmitting cell phone without the S4 sticker caused massive heating up of the head area and the hand that was holding the cell phone. After the same phone had an S4 sticker applied there was a drastic change. There was still some heating up but nothing comparable to the phone without the sticker.

When Walt Silva saw the images he said to me, "This proves you were right."

I asked him what he meant and he said, "These stickers were designed based upon your ability to see and feel energies. The thermography photographs demonstrate that your interpretation of the energies is correct." If I was right then all the other people who claimed to feel the difference in the phones are also right.

We know of many ways to obtain empirical analysis of the effectiveness of the stickers. However, the cost of conducting this kind of research has been beyond our ability to afford.

35. Q. Can S4 Stickers be placed on cell phone covers or do they have to be attached to the phone itself?

A: Yes, the S4 Sticker will have the same effect if it's on either the cell phone itself or the cell phone case and can also just be slid under the case without sticking.

36. Q. If I am wearing a pendant or carrying an S4 sticker, I assume that I am protecting the people around me as well as myself. Can you say anything about how large an area is protected?

A: A certified quantum physicist has stated that Shungite radiates an energy field that goes out many feet depending upon the purity of the Shungite, and they have a way of measuring it beyond our current ability. I would think a distance of 2 feet is a working concept for just the nuggets alone. However, our pendants are energy devices and the energy field would radiate at least that far, and in my opinion at least 6 feet.

37. Q: Does using more than one S4 Sticker increase the protection?

A: On August 21, 2019, the Chicago Tribune newspaper published an article entitled "We tested popular cellphones for radiofrequency radiation. Now the FCC is investigating" by Sam Roe. This article also resulted in a federal class-action lawsuit against Apple and Samsung, because of the results of the test.

The lawyers behind the lawsuit filed simultaneously in California, Illinois, and Iowa. The charges as summarized by The Chicago Tribune on August 29th:

> — alleges that the phone makers "intentionally misrepresented" the safety of their devices, assuring users that the phones had been adequately tested and "were safe to use on and in close proximity to their

bodies."

The complaint, which alleges "negligence, breach of warranty, consumer fraud and unjust enrichment," seeks an unspecified amount of money and medical monitoring for anyone who bought an iPhone 7, iPhone 8, iPhone X, Galaxy S8, Galaxy S9 or Galaxy J3.

Engineer Mark Steele, a British Court Certified authority on electronic devices, stated that to obtain the 500% increase demonstrated by the testing cannot be an accident. That much power increase would have to be built into the device.

The S4 Sticker was designed to attenuate 4G (and below) signals at power emission levels set to a standard known as the Specific Absorption Rate, or SAR, which must be under the federal safety limit. To have it reported that, "phone makers 'intentionally misrepresented' the safety of their devices" that could be 500% over the federal limits of SAR is unnerving at best.

The Shungite Smart Sticker was designed to be used on the Smart Meter and required a more complex sticker with three times the amount of Shungite set in a geometric pattern. With what has now been made public concerning cell phones and that all "Smart Devices" are not what is being advertised, I personally recommend using the Shungite Smart Sticker on all the suspect phones. The S4 Sticker alone will attenuate the signal into biologically compatible energy, but that much unnatural energy, although biologically compatible, is not a good thing. By using extra stickers, either S4 or the Smart Sticker, the field will be imbued with Shungite energy making it more tolerable and more natural.

38. Q. ...why do many say that a pyramid shape is the most effective for the emf blockers?

A: Traditionally, geometric forms are more energetic, with the pyramid being at the top of the list. While Shungite in any form does "block" electromagnetic radiation, the waves still continue to travel around it. Shungite's field, on the other hand, can attenuate signals by causing their fields to reverse rotation to become biologically compatible.

39. Q. Why is there NO change in my meter after adding Shungite Stickers?

A: Meters measuring electric, magnetic or radio frequencies, including WiFi, do not detect the change in the rotation of the EMF/WiFi signal, which is called "attenuation" and results in a harmful signal becoming biocompatible. Shungite stickers do not block or absorb RF energies, otherwise the cell phone would not work well or at all. There is not a meter available to measure this spin change. It is energy-sensitive people who understand what is happening and have developed easy to use products to capitalize on what we observed.

40. Q. Is Bluetooth safe and if not can Shungite help?

A: "Bluetooth radiation has been even less studied than cell phone radiation. The lack of any formal studies has enabled the 'experts' to claim that Bluetooth radiation is safe. This claim is based not on research proving Bluetooth radiation safe, rather on a lack of research proving it to be unsafe – but that is changing quickly." SEE MORE: https://www.rfsafe.com/bluetooth-radiation-dangerous-cell-phone-radiation/

The fact is, Bluetooth safety claims are based upon it NOT being proven unsafe. BUT it has NOT been proven safe. Bluetooth is dangerous because, like regular WiFi, it transmits using Radio Frequency (RF) Radiation.

The Bluetooth device typically emits lower power (and thus it has a short range). However, these devices are normally used for long periods while being secured to the body, such as headphones, earphones, and watches. My advice is to consider these devices just as dangerous as cell phones, especially if the device is a "SMART" device. Use S4 Stickers or, if more practical, we offer Shungite paint that can be dabbed onto a small device.

41. Q. Is fiber-optic safe?

A: **"Fiber-optic cables PRODUCE NO EMF"** – it is light energy, not electromagnetic energy. In fact, because fiberoptic has no EMF, it is used in network cables around MRI equipment in hospitals. Fiber-optic cables are non-metallic", they are made of Lucite or "flexible glass", therefore, NO EMF can come from fiber-optic cables. They can be used to upgrade telecommunications at lower costs and without the inherent dangers posed by conventional communications technology and 5G technology.

42. Q: You said 15 grams of Shungite nuggets would make the electric system become not harmful. Is that still true?

A: We originally were only working with the nuggets and at 15 grams of nuggets the electrical system in a home would change rotation. However, as time passed, we realized Shungite powder was more energetic than nuggets and came up with the Bucky Bandaid.

Then we realized that every secondary electric-powered

motor (because of its wiring) was also creating a toxic energy field. Thus, we recommend that every secondary motor in devices used often, such as hairdryers, vacuum cleaners, and even larger appliances, should also have the Bucky Bandaid.

We recommend S4 magnets for the larger appliances, to obtain energy savings, but the Bucky Bandaid is sufficient to attenuate the electric signals. Another reason for using the S4 magnets and even the S4 Sticker is to create a more intensified Shungite Field within the home. Even when an electrical signal is biocompatible, it is still not a natural energy field. Saturating the fields with Shungite is a more preferable environment.

43. Q: Is a Bucky Bandaid Sticker or three nuggets enough to attenuate the electric system?

A: We assumed that when the electric system in the house was attenuated, all the electrical devices would be emitting energy fields that were also biocompatible. We discovered this was not true. With every **secondary motor**, such as a hairdryer, washing machine, electric stove and any other electrical device, the resulting energy field is in a toxic rotation. **You have to add another Bucky Bandaid to the device (the cheapest option). S4 Stickers and magnets can also be used.**

44. Q: Why do you now say, "There is never enough Shungite"?

A: It was not immediately, but after working with many versions of Shungite from nuggets to various powders and stickers, I began thinking Shungite was doing more than just attenuating EM/WIFI signals. The Shungite energy field morphed the EM/WiFi fields into biocompatible frequencies, but it was still not a natural energy field. A breeze is not destructive but hurricane winds can destroy buildings. There are different amounts of EM/WiFi energies emitted depending upon the device and even on the strength of the WiFi signal. These energies are not natural regardless of being biocompatible.

It became apparent that these unnatural signals could be imbued with the Shungite energy signature. It appears the unnatural EM/WiFi energy fields become carriers of the Shungite field as if the Shungite field was being fueled by the EM/WiFi. This same effect is what I saw with an S4 Shungite Magnet on the refrigerator, which would make the kitchen energy shift drastically to a soothing energy field. The new energy field was a composite of Shungite, magnetic, electric, quantum, and orgone energies.

We have Shungite paint, electric outlet covers, and any of the stickers or magnets that can be used to add Shungite to the home energy fields.

45. Q: What does the Shungite Refrigerator Magnet do?

A: The magnet works with the Shungite field to create an apparent torsion field inside the refrigerator. This enhanced field radiates into the surrounding environment. Inside the refrigerator the food lasts longer and vegetables will tend to wilt and dehydrate instead of getting mushy. It appears that toxins in the food are actually transmuted out of the food and the food is enhanced. With attenuation of the electric system of the refrigerator - particularly older ones - there is more efficiency (the refrigerator will get colder and the thermostat will need to be made warmer). Newer, more efficient refrigerators have a less impressive decrease in electric bills.

45. Q. In a situation with two refrigerators side by side, and a freezer opposite them about 3 feet away, would each appliance need a magnet, or would one magnet cover them all? Or one magnet for the two fridges and one for the freezer?

A: Each one requires a magnet. The key to the magnet is it uses the steel structure of the refrigerator/freezer to create an energy field around and inside the refrigerator.

46. Q. Will Shungite protect me from 5G?

A: No, Shungite cannot protect you from 5G technology. Shungite protects against the technology referred to as 4G that is not the same technology referred to as 5G. See further discussion in the Miscellaneous Section of this chapter.

47. Q: How do I know you can be trusted? I have recently become aware of Shungite and what it is capable of. I am also aware, painfully so, of all the fraud surrounding the emerging "protect yourself from EMF" industry here in the US. I have a basic need to first ensure that what is stated is true and that I am not sending my hard-earned money down some stupid rabbit hole. I would like to try this mineral for myself before spending any money on it. Can you assist me in this regard?

A: I Understand your hesitation. We provide a 100% money back guarantee on all of our products. Out of many thousands of orders less than ten refunds have been requested. We have been in business since May, 2014. In addition, our products are unique and have testimonials and are backed by real science. While we could send you some nuggets or a sticker for you to try, if you do not have critical health problems and are not energy sensitive, you will not feel a difference even if you are being protected. We are real, the dangers are real, and Shungite is real. But you have to come to that conclusion on your own.

A: **By Rod Huff,** a customer and supporter: "1) *You need to briefly peruse the Cosmic Reality web site for a few minutes - essential imo. I can be a smart ass, but in this instance I'm being sincere. The Cosmic Reality database is essential to read before embarking on the Shungite voyage. 2). You need to go to math class and do your math homework if you want to utilize math in your life. Same goes for Shungite imo. This is step 1 of an incredible Shungite Shaman journey. IMO you can't skip step 1.*"

C60 MOLECULES

48. Q: How many C60 molecules are in a Shungite nugget?

A: It depends on where in the Mother Lode the nugget was mined. Within the Karelian Shungite field, there are different amounts of carbon. The more carbon the more chance of having C60 molecules. But even with zero fullerenes the Shungite still does the same job. I know that sounds wrong because we place so much emphasis on the C60 molecule and it being the explanation for the magic of Shungite. The fact is, even the smallest fleck of Shungite does what is claimed. Every fleck of Shungite is attached to all other flecks due to Quantum Entanglement. Elite/Noble Shungite, because of high carbon content, has the most C60 molecules. Whether or not a C60 molecule is in a particle of Shungite, the signature energy field of Shungite is the same.

49. Q: Is C60 in Shungite the same as laboratory

created C60?

A: Absolutely not. The C60 in Shungite was created during the time it took for the Shungite to be created in outer space and then to travel to Earth. Shungite C60 is imbued with energies of a cosmic source. Lab-made C60 is just that; something made in a laboratory. At the 3D level, both types may appear and act similarly but at the energetic levels there is no comparison.

SHUNGITE WEAVE AND THE SHUNGITE WORLD GRID

50. Q: What is the Shungite Weave?

A: Every piece of the Karelian Shungite deposit is linked to every other piece. Whether or not a C60 molecule is in a particle of Shungite, the signature energy field of Shungite is the same. That energy field now encompasses the entire planet and is referred to as the "Shungite Weave". Shungite works whether or not it has a C60 molecule because of this connection. There are weaves of pine trees, and coconut trees etc., that all belong to the bigger energy weave of the "Tree Weave". There is a "Water Weave" and a weave for every version of life.

51. Q: What is the Shungite World Grid?

A: This is a project where individuals place Shungite nuggets and/or devices in areas they are inspired to gift with Shungite. By doing this we are tying in with the Shungite Weave while creating a secondary weave incorporating human thought focused on gifting Shungite to the Environment. Search "Shungite World Grid".

ROUNDUP, MOLD & OTHER TOXINS VS SHUNGITE

52. Q: Can Shungite destroy Glyphosate (Roundup)?

A: We do not have empirical proof that Shungite works on glyphosate in the same way it works on other toxins. This kind of research is beyond our financial ability to conduct at this time. However, we have a story that shows this...if you believe that metaphysical observations can be accurate. Here is the story:

Janet had 7 acres she leased out only for the growing of hay. Her old tenant retired from farming and the new tenant was growing hay. Now, who would imagine that you are growing hay and you decide to put Roundup on it? I am not sure I ever heard how Janet found out this had been done, but when she realized it, she was in a total meltdown. Janet knew, from alternative news, that the claim by the industry that the glyphosate in Roundup disappears within a few days or a couple of weeks was bogus. Maybe she had read something like this:

> "Glyphosate was initially thought to break down in the soil very quickly. Researchers thought it was gone because they couldn't find it by itself in the soil, but now we know that it persists by binding with essential nutrients. Soil biology does eventually degrade glyphosate, but researchers think it takes a while. One study showed Roundup persisting in clay soils for over 20 years." - https://farmingsweetbay.wordpress.com/2011/12/17/getting-roundup-out-of-our-farms-soil/

The only hope Janet had was to use Shungite. She walked around the 7 acres dropping Shungite nuggets along its edges. She knew about us and talked to Derek asking, "Will this work?" Derek said yes. But Janet asked to also speak with me.

Janet could have gotten chemical analysis costing $1000 for a chemical test for glyphosate. But one test would not have provided proof, as she would have to know exactly where the chemical could be located within the 7 acres. I suggested she find someone who does muscle testing, which would allow many tests to be conducted over the 7 acres.

What is muscle testing? Those knowledgeable about energy healing use muscle testing as a way of diagnosing the health of the body. It can also be used to determine how the body is responding to stimuli from the environment or other elements such as food to detect food allergies. For those not familiar with the basics of energy healing, this undoubtedly sounds "woo woo". From the standpoint of enerology it makes complete sense. The bioelectromagnetic fields of energy that comprise the blueprint of the physical body have a vast potential for providing information on every aspect of the physical body. Tapping into the information is done by many energy healers in many ways including muscle testing, which is also referred to as applied kinesiology or biomechanics.

Janet knew someone who used muscle testing in her practice. When this woman tested for toxins in the soil, the muscle testing indicated there were none.

There was also a small stream running through the property. Janet took two containers of water from the stream. In one container she put 3 Shungite nuggets (making sure to keep the containers away from each other). Muscle testing showed the Shungite Energized Water was pure but the other water was toxic.

Janet took the nuggets out of the one container and dropped them in the toxic water. Immediately they did another muscle test. The tester was totally stunned when the water that was toxic a few minutes before was now pure from the addition of 3 black stones.

53. Q: Can Shungite eliminate Mold and Biofilm?

A: Jason Tetro, microbiologist, and author of *The Germ Files* states that there are two types of mold. One type is mold spores in the water itself, the second is biofilm easily seen in dog water bowls as a slick, oil like film on the sides of the bowl. The same biofilm can come from a human mouth and be left in whatever water container you are using. Add warmth to the humid environment containing either mold type and you will have mold growth. Add sugar and the growth will accelerate.

We have had three reports of mold growing in Shungite water/Shungite Energized Water. We continually have confirmation that the biofilm in animal water bowls does NOT happen when three Shungite nuggets are in the bowl.

One complaint about mold was in Shungite Energized sweet tea, another was in the cracks of a porcelain container, and the third in a reusable container left for days uncleaned. It is unlikely these are caused by biofilm but mold spores in the water could be the cause. It is not the mold but the mycotoxins it creates that are toxic to humans and animals. My opinion is the mold seen in these situations may have been there but the mycotoxins were probably not there. More research is required.

54. Q: Why do I have Algae in my Shungite swimming pool?

A: Algae grow in water and are therefore aquatic organisms that have the same ability as plants have to conduct photosynthesis (creating carbohydrates out of sunlight).

There are vast numbers of algae and some are critical to our existence. Half of the oxygen in the atmosphere is produced by algae and they are the source of food for other aquatic organisms. It is not surprising that two swimming pool owners reported algae actually becoming more of a problem upon adding Shungite to the pool. Some algae would not be affected by a Shungite field as they are not toxic molecules nor toxic organisms. Algae "blooms" or excessive growth is a result of nutrient pollution, where an excess of nitrogen and phosphorus stimulate algae into unrestrained growth.

Except for the two reports of algae in a pool with Shungite, all the other reports indicate Shungite does for swimming pools what it does for drinking water. This is another subject requiring more research.

ELITE/NOBLE VS. REGULAR SHUNGITE

55. Q: What is the difference between Elite, Noble and Regular Shungite?

A: The regular, Grade B/2 or what we call "Raw" Shungite that we use produces an energy field more compatible with the 3D, such as your body. Elite simply has a different energy that many prefer for whatever reason.

The best I can figure out is that when "Elite" is used the Shungite has a brownish color whereas "Noble" is on the dark black side and may be another name for "Petrovsky" Shungite. By any name it is the same basic mineral makeup and we will only refer to it as Elite Shungite. Elite is mined by hand because it is found as veins within the Shungite field and is relatively fragile. It is very costly to mine and therefore the first to be targeted by fraudulent people. I have compared Elite to two common coal types,

Anthracite and Bituminous. I could not find anything visual to distinguish the Elite from the coal.

We do not sell this "Grade A Shungite' in any form and all our science is based upon the "regular" or "Raw" Shungite. Essentially, the darker black the stone the more carbon, and more carbon indicates more C60 Fullerenes.

But C60 is only one component of a very specific mix of minerals and cosmic energies. There is a "Quantum Entanglement" with Shungite that links every single particle of it back to the Mother Lode in Karelia. Whether or not your Shungite has a million C60 molecules or none - its effects worldwide are the same.

"Quantum entanglement is a physical phenomenon that occurs when pairs or groups of particles are generated, interact, or share spatial proximity in ways such that the quantum state of each particle cannot be described independently of the state of the other(s), even when the particles are separated by a large distance."

PENDANTS

56. Q: Under the Cosmic Silver Enhanced Pendants section there are several differently-priced options from $105 - $175. If the silver-enhancing technology is the same for all of them, what is the reason for the difference in price? Size of Nugget?

A: It is the size of the nugget. And I will point out that with Shungite, bigger is not necessarily better. However, some people just like more Shungite. The reason Cosmic Silver pendants are more expensive is that nano silver is embedded on the surface during tumbling with pure silver. The silver migrates into the nugget. Obviously, the larger the nugget, the larger the amount of silver covering it. Thus, much of the price difference is due to the amount of silver going into the Shungite.

57. Q: Can a person wear or surround themselves with TOO much shungite? For example: Can I wear a bracelet, necklace and put it in my shoes? And can I also sleep with nuggets in my pillows, and drink the water without negative effects or are all of them canceling each other out?

A: There is never enough Shungite and Shungite links up with all other Shungite to create a more coherent energy field. It is the same reason we suggest always using at least 3 Shungite nuggets for most applications.

58. Q: How is a wire wrapped pendant made?

A: The Shungite wire wrapped pendants we produce are Energy Devices worn as a pendant. To be able to wrap them you have to be energy sensitive. Orgone Energy flows through the wire in one direction. Energy also flows through the nugget in one direction. You have to be able to determine the flow of energy to merge the Orgone and Shungite energy so they are both flowing in the same direction and that must be from the ground up. As far as wire thickness is concerned, it must be no smaller than 18 gauge and it should not be a silver-coated wire or silver wire, as the silver will migrate off the wire and into the Shungite, unless you want that to happen.

59. Q: Why do you say your wrapped pendant is an energy device?

A: The wire attracts an energy called "orgone", as discovered by Wilhelm Reich. Orgone energy has been called prana, life force, ki, chi, mana, universal energy, the Source... essentially the life force of the Universe. When I stated that energy flows through the wire, the energy is orgone. That is why it is important to be able to feel which direction the orgone is flowing. You want the orgone and Shungite energy to be flowing in the same direction. We wrap the pendants so the combined energy field is moving from the ground upward. The combined energy field works with bioelectromagnetic systems to create balance and stability. Your energy bodies become healthier and they comprise the blueprint for the physical body.

60. Q: What is the difference between the wire-wrapped pendant and a Cosmic Silver pendant?

A: Both pendants are wire wrapped as explained above. It is the nugget that is different. Early on we discovered that silver-infused Shungite created a more stable energy field. At the quantum level, what we call Silver Saturated Shungite connects to the quantum field and keeps the connection open. Raw Shungite, on the other hand, makes the connection in a pulsing manner, as if the door to the quantum field opens and shuts. Nuggets are put into a tumbler with silver and without the sand or grit normally used in tumbling stones. They are tumbled for three days until a layer of silver coats the nuggets and in fact infuses the silver into the Shungite.

Wire wrapped pendants with raw nuggets are less able to attenuate and produce biocompatible WiFi signals. Wrapped raw pendants used for animals that are in a Shungite environment are fine. Most humans, who have to go out into the real world that is without the protection of Shungite, should be using the wire wrapped Cosmic Silver pendant. The Cosmic Silver pendant is able to attenuate WiFi signals you may encounter anywhere outside a Shungite environment. Both pendants will balance and stabilize bioelectromagnetic energy fields.

61. Q: How do I care for my Shungite Pendant?

A: Regardless of which pendant you choose, you do not have to "recharge or clean" them, other than washing them off. It is perfectly safe to wear them in the shower or swimming.

62. Q: What is the difference between the pendant and the bracelets?

A: Every Shungite bead has its own energy field. Three beads will create a more coherent field. So a Shungite beaded bracelet is inherently more energetic than one raw nugget. There is also a current of orgone running through them. However, the orgone flow is vastly stronger in a wire wrapped nugget than in a bracelet of beads. The bottom line when choosing which one to use is what feels better to you. Or wear them both.

SHUNGITE POWDER

63. Q: What is the powder used for and is there more than one type of Shungite powder?

A: Shungite powder is collected during the processing of Shungite, such as sorting the sizes of nuggets. The powder is collected and sold. As it is based on Raw Shungite we call it Raw Shungite Powder. We also create saturated Silver Shungite Powder called "S4 Powder" directly out of the commercial Raw Powder. Typically the powder is used in gardens, added to salves/balms/lotions and in the making of energy devices. It is sold from the mine in different sizes from fine to coarse.

64. Q: What is the best way to use Shungite in the garden?

A: You need a garden sprayer that attaches to a hose or is one you simply fill up. In either case, you can use three nuggets or a small amount of powder. We recommend the powder because you are actually sprinkling particles of Shungite that will continue radiating the field. Shungite Energized water, if you are using it daily, is fine, but without being in the Shungite field, water on the garden will eventually lose its Shungite spin. How much powder to use is dependent upon how much power is behind the hose and/or how fast it feeds out of the container. The bottom line is you do not need much to get the effects, but the more the better. You can also just place nuggets around the garden.

65. Q: Can Shungite powder be ingested?

A: We work with Raw Shungite powder and the Shungite S4/Raw powder mix called "Shungite Bee Powder". We do not recommend ingestion for obvious legal reasons. Even though we can certify our Shungite Powder is from the Karelian mines, the processing does not have "food quality" as a goal. When we have honey products with added powder, the powder used is obtained from the nuggets themselves, as surface powder is always at the bottom of the containers. In our products, there is a very small pinch of powder. You do not need to ingest the powder to obtain the benefits of Shungite. Is ingesting an added benefit? Perhaps, and if you choose to go there think in terms of each particle of powder being equivalent to a nugget.

66. Q: How is Shungite powder used in health products?

A: Take your favorite skin softener, moisturizer, wound ointment and simply add a small amount of powder depending upon the size of the container. In a 2 oz bottle, this would be a "dash" of powder. Shungite likes energy fields and as long as you are using natural ingredients (each with their own energy signature) the Shungite will enhance their properties.

MAGNETS

67. Q: How are your magnets made?

A: Liquid plastic called resin mixed with S4 and Raw Shungite powder is poured into a mold and a neodymium rare earth magnet is added. The magnet is positioned with the north side of the magnet on the bottom. It is the north side that needs to be attached to the metal in the refrigerator, automobile, or anyplace else the magnet is attached. We have two types of magnets. One has a low profile we recommend for use in an automobile, but the various versions are interchangeable.

68. Q: What do the magnets do for a refrigerator?

A: On appliances, the combination of Shungite and magnetic energy connect to the Quantum Field and also to the electric system. Also, always present is the field of orgone energy. The combined fields create a spinning energy field inside the appliance that radiates out into the surrounding environment for at least six feet.

Studies developing the concept of torsion fields begun by Russian scientist Nikolai Kozyrev (1908-1983) have gone from being ridiculed to being accepted as serious scientific inquiry. It is likely that the spinning energy field created by a Shungite magnet on the refrigerator is a torsion field.

This field attenuates all EM/WiFi signals associated with the refrigerator. One result is that the appliance runs more efficiently. Not only is there less electric usage, the gas used to create the cold temperatures is purified, allowing it to work more efficiently. In fact, you normally have to turn down the cold setting, as the increased efficiency results in the refrigerators being too cold, causing vegetables to freeze.

Inside the refrigerator, the energy field has similar effects to the energy fields discovered to be associated with pyramids. In a pyramid field, food is enhanced, with slower rotting and things do not turn into mush, as they seem to dehydrate. The same effects are observed in a Shungite refrigerator. An almost empty container of Half-and-Half (half cream and half milk) was still good six months after its expiration date.

69. Q: What do the magnets do for an automobile?

A: The steel frame of automobiles acts like a refrigerator with a Shungite magnet. The combined energy field of Shungite, orgone, electric and electronic signals, and the quantum field creates an envelope of protection inside the car against EM/WiFi signals and airborne toxins. It also takes impurities out of the gas and oil allowing for increased efficiency and higher gas mileage.

70. Q: How do I attach the magnet?

A: Always put the north side of the magnet against the appliance and any part of the car that is metal. In the newer cars with an amazing amount of plastic, finding metal to attract the magnet can be problematic. Door frames, the sliding brackets holding seats, and areas of exposed metal, like where the spare tire is stored, are typically connected directly to the steel car frame. See the Cosmic Reality website for pictures showing which side is north.

71. Q: Does it matter which side of the magnet is

attached to the refrigerator?

A: Yes! To get the beneficial torsion field inside the refrigerator, the north side of the magnet must be the point of attachment. See the Cosmic Reality website for pictures showing which side is north.

72. Q: Does it matter where I place the magnet?

A: Placing a magnet, whether on a refrigerator or other electric device, or an automobile, requires the north side of the magnet to be on the metal. In some refrigerators, the stainless steel exterior prevents the magnet attaching. We recommend you find someplace, even on the bottom or the back, where you can find metal to attach the magnet. We do not have enough information regarding what happens if you put it inside the refrigerator, but you can try it and hopefully report back. Does your food last longer? Is the refrigerator running more efficiently so you had to turn down the thermostat? Does your food taste better? In a car that has a lot of plastic, you still have to find metal. Along the sides of doors, the tracks holding the seats, or the area where the spare tire is stored is where you are likely to find metal.

73. Q: Is one magnet enough?

A: To provide basic protection and enhancement of refrigerated foods, one Shungite magnet is sufficient. To optimize energy savings and intensify the overall positive energy environment you can add up to three magnets. With more than three there is no notable change in energy savings.

There is never enough Shungite. When first starting out, I looked to find the least amount of Shungite that can reverse the spin to create biocompatible EM signals. Our products are based on that goal. Still, there are other problems, like the electric system wires and outlets all radiating a field of EM radiation that is NOT natural. Shungite may make the signals biocompatible but they are still detrimental, although to a much lesser degree, because of the amount of unnatural energy you are being subjected to. If Shungite is added throughout the system, the biocompatable frequencies are enhanced. As the magnets are the most energetic way of introducing the combined fields, adding magnets to appliances will be beneficial but not necessary.

74. Q: Are there other uses for the magnets besides refrigerators and automobiles?

A: Shungite magnets can also be used on large appliances to make them more efficient and to spread the Shungite energy field. One good place is the hot water heater. This helps with energy efficiency and creates Shungite Energized Water inside the tank. A Shungite magnet on the natural gas intake pipe or the oil tank used for heating will take the impurities out of the gas or heating oil for more efficient burning.

MISCELLANEOUS

75. Q: What is the range of one Shungite nugget vs three Shungite nuggets?

A: We do not have empirical measurements. We tell people to think of the energy field of a single nugget as extending to 4 feet but I suspect it is much larger. A certified quantum physicist said they had measured the field using some tech equipment, and to be honest I did not know what he was talking about. He also said it depended upon the quality of the nugget. It was an odd conversation as he pioneered a product that is based on Shungite but never let that be known to me until he retired as President of the company. He confirmed our science only by direct questioning.

==Three nuggets create a secondary field that radiates out farther and Walt determined it was 7 feet. He also determined the nuggets must be within 2 feet of each other for the coherent field to engage.==

76. Q: What do you mean when you talk about the 3-6-9 principle?

> "If you only knew the magnificence of the three, the six and the nine... then you would have a key to the universe." -Nikola Tesla

A: Many have tried explaining Tesla's statement, with many conjectures. In our case, we were directed by guides to always use three nuggets. Walt had done a shamanic journey and connected with guides concerning Shungite. They said the three nuggets created a "coherent field".

I did not pay attention to it. Then, while being a passenger in a car traveling down the highway through downtown Miami, my attention was drawn to this huge billboard. It was completely white with black lettering: **THREE IS COHERENT**. I am sure I was the only one to see it. The spiritual guides gently leading us down the Shungite path can be very persistent. So we began recommending three nuggets because we were told to, LOL.

So, about three years go by and we are gifted Kirlian photographs of Shungite by Sofiya Blank, the Russian scientist who took them. Kirlian Photography is a technique that is able to catch subtle energy fields as a photograph. In the photograph you can see the energy fields of the different geometric forms made out of Shungite. What you can also see is a secondary field connecting three of them. That secondary field is the coherent field. What is it? Well, the opposite of coherent is incoherent and we know what that means.

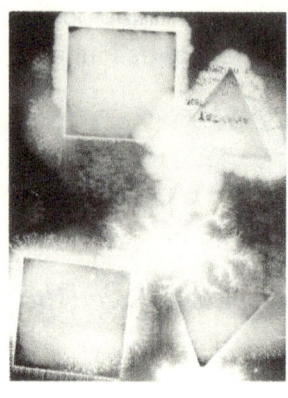

Then Derek Condit started the World Shungite Grid by driving 4,000 miles and throwing Shungite out the window. This began a trend and today there are over 129,083 views of the map locating places where people have gifted Shungite to nature. Many knew the rule of three nuggets and we began realizing that if you placed three nuggets near another grouping of three nuggets an energetic connection manifested. And when you added a third group of three, another even more energetic stable energy field was created.

77. Q: Does Shungite heal?

A: We make two claims regarding Shungite healing. The first is that in a Shungite environment and its attenuation of EM/WiFi signals, all biological forms from humans to plants will be healthier, and overall health will be enhanced with Shungite Energized Water eliminating toxins and spinning the water to make it more useable by the physical cells.

The second claim is that Shungite can stabilize and break down energy blockages in the bioelectromagnetic bodies of animals and humans. This allows for physical healing. Simply getting into a Shungite environment and using

Shungite personal protection energy devices, such as our wrapped pendants, helps people heal because their energy bodies are being enhanced. People using many modalities of energy healing find Shungite enhances their efforts.

We do not make claims of specific healing attributed to Shungite. What we do is report observations and stories from our customers. All we do is supply a variety of energy devices created by using Shungite in a multitude of ways. It is up to the individual to decide what is right for them. Please see Chapter 2 for Customer testimonials.

78. Q: Is it true Shungite phones can be used as a healing device?

A: This concept came from customer testimonials. They did have stories of apparent beneficial results by using a Shungite cellphone to send healing energy. There were a few of these reports for different healing situations. However, there are simply too many variables at play to feel safe recommending electronic devices with Shungite be used as a healing modality. I would still be very cautious. In the Fall of 2019 Apple and Samsung were sued for having phones 500% over the Federal SAR levels indicating how much radiation can be emitted. Even attenuated, those signals are very powerful and not natural. A cautionary message.

79. Q: What are the side effects of using shungite?

A: Shungite balances and stabilizes bioelectromagnetic energy fields. The more adjustment required will result in a more profound reaction to being introduced to Shungite. Some people go through a detoxing process. Others find they are compelled to make life changes. It is likely these changes are what is needed, and may be a result of being able to think more clearly as the EM/WiFi fog leaves the brain. The fog is caused by inflammation resulting from heating of the brain from EM/WiFi that is not biocompatible.

80. Q: Why hasn't shungite been more mainstreamed, exposed in the West, if its so beneficial?

A: The short answer is money. There was not a lot of money to be made. Shungite was known as a water purifier and the nuggets were dirt cheap. Any health benefits were attributable to the fact that the Shungite water was pure and therefore beneficial to health. It was not until Regina Martino and her book *Shungite: Protection, Healing, and Detoxification* discussed the benefits Shungite provided to the energy bodies and therefore improved health that Shungite got attention in Europe. Her book was not published in English until after we began talking about it on internet radio. As our customers began relating health benefits that we passed on to our listeners, Shungite began trending.

It is ironic that Shungite did not get attention in Russia until 1985 when it was discovered it contained the C60 molecule. It appears university level scientists began to research the water purification effects and soon found the health benefits.

The concept that Shungite can attenuate EM/WiFi and mitigate their dangers is directly attributable to me. I got on to this profound capability of Shungite because the Russian Military was using it to shield electronics against Electro-Magnet Pulses resulting from the detonation of nuclear devices.

81. Q: What do you mean by "attenuate"?

A: Attenuate came to my attention in a Russian document

translated directly into English from Russian. Normally, what was available as an English translation was not directly from the Russian. Most documents in English talking about Shungite, that were originally written in Russian, had been translated from French, German and Spanish documents. The typical used terms of "Shungite blocks" or "absorbs" was replaced by "Shungite attenuates".

The definitions of attenuate in Enerology are:

> 1. To change an electromagnetic signal so that it becomes biocompatible by reversal of the signal's rotation.
>
> 2. The reversal of spin in a toxic molecule that will lose molecular cohesion and fall apart into atoms.

82. Q: What do you mean by Shungite sentience?

A: For the purposes of working with Shungite, the Metaphysical definition comes into play. In Eastern philosophy, sentience is a metaphysical quality of all things that require respect and care. Shungite interacts with thought energy and will respond. The more you engage your imagination while working with Shungite, the more you can learn about its properties.

83. Q: What is Shungite Rubber?

A: It is rubber mixed with S4 and Raw Shungite Powder. It is made into various shapes and sizes for many purposes, including putting in shoes, sleeping and sitting on it, and it has been recently made into wheelchair covers.

As the Earth shifts into a new state, with new ways of thinking and feeling, this has brought forth tools for the paradigm of the New Energy, where we can address the state of the "intangible" vibrations that surround us every day.

The new tools are the product of combining the energy attributes and properties of geometric bodies (such as pyramids and cones) with materials that work to attract, transmute and counteract "stagnant" and "depleting" energy from a living or work space.

These can be, and have been used for energy work and other kinds of healing work.

- Walt Silva, NewParadigmTools.net

Chapter 4

Enerology and Shungite Science

THE UNIVERSE OF SPIRITUAL INTERVENTION (USI)

When all is said and done, the fundamental principle of Enerology is we are not alone. We are continually being guided, whether it be from our soul and higher consciousness or angelic and spiritual beings of higher consciousness, I simply call it The Universe of Spiritual Intervention (USI). My current age is 71 and it affords me the ability to look back over seven decades to see the intricately woven tapestry of my own life. I can honestly say, every step of the way was guided by information that simply popped into my head and by the continual synchronicities that brought people, thoughts, and experiences into my path. I suspect the USI is at work in every person's life whether they acknowledge it or not.

The information I am about to present is mine, in that I processed it and am writing about it. It is uniquely my perspective on reality. But it is a reality that I was guided to understand by the USI.

VIBRATIONAL MEDICINE

The experience I acquired as a U.S. Army Electronic Warfare Officer provided me with the ability to think of electro-magnetic energy, fields, waves, and signals as tangible, physical aspects of a physical universe. On the battlefield, energy is used for communication, radar detection, weapon guidance, and air traffic control. An enemy can use those same invisible signals to identify, locate, spy-on, and destroy opposing military forces. Energy terminology includes "Electronic Warfare" and "Electronic Battlefields".

Vibrational Medicine is a growing field of thought, recognizing human and animal bodies as energy battlefields, where energy warfare can fight off attacks by infections, toxic buildup, trauma, and even aging itself. (See Vibrational Medicine by Dr. Richard Gerber.)

This is not a new concept in the Art of Healing. Psychic healers, herbalists, homeopathic doctors, and acupuncturists have been using energy to heal for many thousands of years. What is new about the subject is the growing body of qualitative proof by the orthodox scientific community concerning numerous claims and aspects of Vibrational Medicine.

The key to vibrational medicine lies in accepting the multilayered, energetic anatomy of the human being. Your "space" is not just that contained within your physical body. In reality, your body is one aspect of a multilayered entity operating within the positive space/time continuum. The other aspects of your true being lie in the negative time/space continuum and appear to be invisible to the physical universe because they are operating at speeds in excess of the speed of light.

Quantum Physics has proven the existence of faster than light energies by using complicated measuring devices that analyze the effects of these invisible energies on the physical plane. We also have surmised the existence of other energy bodies within our multi-layered anatomies by observing the impact such bodies have upon us. We cannot see or touch the soul with our limited perceptions, but there are more of us who believe in the existence of a soul than those who do not believe.

The most commonly known subtle body is the "astral" body. It is supposedly the energetic level that is linked to appetites and emotions.

Another energetic body believed to exist is the "mental" body. The scientific support of the existence of this body has gained popularity and is called "The Mind-Body Connection", and while this energy body has a profound effect on your health, it is the "etheric" body that is directly affected by Shungite.

The subtle body having the most scientific backup is called the "etheric" body. The etheric body is the subtle body most closely aligned to the frequency of the physical dimension. The etheric body provides the "energetic blueprint" formulating our very bodies. At the cellular level, the etheric and physical bodies actually share the same cells.

To understand how two separate yet interconnected energy bodies can share the same cells, we can use the television as an example. Each television station transmits a signal, which can be received by your television. All signals are received continuously and simultaneously. The only thing you change within the television is the tuner - a device allowing only one unique frequency to be seen and heard. Yet regardless of which signal is chosen, all signals are viewed upon the same screen. The screen is a shared mechanism.

The cells we perceive as being physical, are continuously and simultaneously shared by both the physical and etheric bodies. And each body has its own frequency systems, which interface with cells. In the physical body, there are circulatory, nervous, muscular, and other physical systems.

The etheric body has its own unique systems.

The physical body surrounds cells in a fluid that has the ability to detect abnormal cells, viruses, and bacteria that should not be there. Antibodies are sent to fight these unwanted elements and the immune system is doing its job.

The corresponding etheric system that detects cell abnormalities begins with the ethereal fluidium - a part of the etheric body surrounding every cell. It is surmised that the ethereal fluidium is capable of transmitting a warning to the etheric body when the cells are unbalanced in their energies.

Instead of sending out "antibodies", the etheric body intensifies its output of "vital energy", also called the "life force", to those unbalanced areas. Thus, in an acute state of illness, the human being is fighting the disease with the physical body's immune system and the etheric body's intensification of nutritive energy.

The physical body is continually being monitored and provided with the necessary energy to overcome the damaging effects of emotional depression, physical stress, chemical toxicity, nutritional deficiencies, viral or bacterial infections, and physical trauma. This perfect scenario predisposes two elements: first, the etheric body can provide necessary additional nutritive energy; and secondly, the etheric body gets the warning that something has gone wrong.

Obviously, if there is massive damage to the physical cells, regardless of the health of the etheric body, there may be no way for the etheric body to generate sufficient energy to overcome such damage. In a very weakened etheric condition, even small energy requirements can overpower the etheric body's defenses.

Energy Healing

If the hypothesis that the physical body is, in fact, an energy body is correct, suppose you could figure out the exact type of energy required to bring that physical body back to the state of balance and health? Energy healers from "New Age" to "Witch Doctor" have been demonstrating healing through energy alone. Jesus is a great example of energy healing. He did not say, "Take this drug." His "miracles" were based upon energy transference. Jesus seemed able to manifest a universal healing frequency.

Some healers also seem to tap into a universal energy capable of healing a multitude of ailments. One of those modalities is called Reiki. People designated Reiki Masters are able to tune into a frequency of universal healing, which can be transferred by thought alone, or through the human touch, to others. By 2019, Reiki is being used in a number of hospitals all over the world in conjunction with establishment medicine including one Mexican hospital, three US cancer hospitals, Spanish hospitals in Madrid, Barcelona, Seville, and Valencia, and healthcare facilities in the United Kingdom, Canada, Brazil, Chile, Argentina, and Australia.

Reiki is only one of many types of energy exchanges from one human to another being used. Jesus and his touch imparting healing is probably the best known among the vast number of medicine men, shamans or healers throughout the world since time began. With advances in measuring devices capable of mapping energy activities in the brain, we can see that Reiki masters show a marked change in their brains and similar changes are seen in their patients. But hands-on healers are not easy to find.

Acupuncture is an ancient Chinese technique that stimulates points on the skin, called acupoints, with needles. This is a direct manual stimulation of the physical body's energy system as the acupoints connect to the meridian system identified as an energy system within the body. There is growing scientific validation that the meridian system, chakra system, and other energy fields exist. For thousands of years acupuncture has been an accepted healing technique that continues today. Massaging alone may also stimulate the energy system.

Herbal: Some energy healers work with plants and the healing potential of many plants is truly magical. Some say herb healing is a result of chemicals in the herb carrying the healing properties. Enerology would contend it is not the chemical itself but the energy being carried by the herb. Others claim that the energy alone in crystals and other minerals has healing capabilities.

For any of this energy healing to work, you need to be able to manifest either a universal healing energy or identify the specific energy needed and then find a way to administer it. Diagnosing the problem and the cure are obviously critical.

The key is figuring out what is energetically unbalanced and what energy would correct the imbalance, either at the etheric or the physical energy levels. Just as important as diagnosis and identification of the energy field required for healing, is identifying how you deliver the energy and in what form. Do you use herbs, crystals, acupuncture, energy transfer from the healer to the client, or do you look at treatments that create the required healing energies?

Homeopathy is a system of alternative medicine created in 1796 by Samuel Hahnemann. The concept is based on the belief that the body can cure itself. Those who practice homeopathy use tiny amounts of various parts of plants mixed in water.

This is what is really weird. They take a sample from a plant, like a small slice of the leaf. They put that into a small amount of water. To make a stronger solution they take a few drops of that first mixture and add it to another small amount of water. Every time this is done the resulting solution is numbered. So you start with 1 and do it 5 more times to get a 6X or a solution that is 6 times as strong, but after the first solution there is nothing material (3D or physical) in the solution! Essentially, it is water carrying the vibration of the original sample. And the more times you do this, the stronger the effect. Thus 6X is more powerful than 2X.

It sounds really nutty. But the cure rate was so high, homeopathic doctors worked in American hospitals until the American Medical Association (AMA) was established in 1847. The AMA, created by other than alternative physicians, cleared out those successful doctors with high rates in making people feel better, called them charlatans, sent them on their way, and ushered in what has become known as "Big Pharma".

SYMPATHETIC RESONANCE

Homeopathy is based on the concept that in today's medical jargon is called the "Mind-Body Connection". It really can be simplified as "the body can cure itself". While the basic concept of what is behind homeopathy is that "like cures like", the true source of the magic is in the concept of sympathetic resonance.

Everything is made of energy and what we perceive as the physical universe is comprised of energy forms vibrating within the same basic frequencies. It results in the concept of "frozen energy" where similar vibrations look physical and we call it "material matter".

Within the physical 3D reality, sympathetic resonance occurs between things having identical or very similar energy fields. Tuning forks and the wires of string instruments most easily demonstrate resonance. One tuning fork is hit setting up a sound vibration and another identical tuning fork begins sounding even without a physical hit to start it humming. Play a guitar string and a guitar feet away will have the same string resonate.

So, in homeopathic medicine, a person's symptoms are matched with what can be brought on by a specific plant. When you have a cold with that runny nose and those watery eyes, take some homeopathic Allium cepa which is found in onions. And what do onions do? Make your eyes water and therefore your nose runs. This is sympathetic resonance at play. By adding the energy signature identical to the symptoms (homeopathic medicine only carries energy signatures and no molecules of the original plant), the symptoms lessen or disappear.

I honestly cannot explain why homeopathy works, but it all starts with similar energies creating a sympathetic resonance. Perhaps it simply becomes a signal alerting the body's immune system that there is a problem. But I suspect it is more. Let's take a look at other healing modalities, to see if there is an answer there.

Energy Healing Devices

My first really in-depth exposure to the concepts of energy healing came around 1989 when Dr. Richard Gerber published his textbook entitled *Vibrational Medicine*. That book is still in print in an updated version and is, in fact, the best collection of research on the concept of energy healing and that we are energy beings that I have personally come across. If it is really studied, it presents well-documented research supporting the concept of "vibrational medicine".

The concept is simple. We are energy beings with the physical body appearing to be made of physical material. But physical matter is just an energy layer that appears frozen to us because we are all vibrating within the same 3D frequency spectrum. If we view the physical body as a form of energy, then with energy tuning and adjustments physical healing can be accomplished.

Even back when Dr. Gerber published the 1989 book, there were a number of machines capable of reading the bioelectromagnetic fields to determine a person's health, and, where there is an energy problem, determine what energies they need to regain health. In 2019 there are many other ways of doing the same thing. In fact, there are so many of them it is very difficult to know what really works for you. But each of these machines matches specific diseases with energies discovered through research that could counteract the disease.

After being looked at for decades, one 2019 YouTube video called **"We've Found the Magic Frequency"** went viral. The video claimed they could cure cancer with energy alone. An abstract published by the US National Library of Medicine entitled "Targeted treatment of cancer with radiofrequency electromagnetic fields amplitude-modulated at tumor-specific frequencies" in its conclusions states:

> *In summary, our clinical results provide strong evidence that the intrabuccal administration of RF EMF amplitude-*

> *modulated at tumor-specific frequencies is safe and well-tolerated and may lead to long lasting therapeutic responses in patients with advanced cancer. Our in vitro experiments demonstrate that cancer cell proliferation can be targeted using tumor-specific modulation frequencies, which were identified in patients diagnosed with cancer. Tumor-specific modulation frequencies block the growth of cancer cells, modify gene expression, and disrupt the mitotic spindle.* - Chin J Cancer. 2013 Nov; 32(11): 573–581 PMCID: PMC3845545

Wow! This takes the subtle energetic healing of homeopathy to a totally new level. Instead of adding beneficial healing frequencies homeopathically they can manipulate a frequency to destroy a specific microorganism and specific cells!

Am I surprised? No, because of a man named Raymond Royal Rife.

Raymond Royal Rife (1888-1971)

Rife is known for his work in imaging and medical microscopy. Starting with prisms to isolate various light colors into radio frequencies, Rife built complicated equipment that allowed living microorganisms to be viewed and studied. Rife's microscope used monochromatic light that caused the organism to fluoresce. Rife could identify the virus he was observing by the color it refracted.

Rife was able to observe living viruses in action attacking living cells. He **determined that each life form had a specific resonant frequency**. In fact, he was able to isolate and discover that, yes, there were specific viruses that induce the creation of tumors in the body. **Rife also believed that using the concept of resonance, unwanted organisms could be destroyed by energy without damaging anything else.** It was very specific energy targeting one type of virus.

The energy was delivered using a radio frequency wave emitted by a gas within a glass tube. This signal was readily accepted by the body and, according to Rife's records, he successful eradicated microorganisms including anthrax, cholera, tetanus, B. coli, influenza, spinal meningitis, tuberculosis, pneumonia, syphilis, gonorrhea, leprosy, streptococcus, conjunctivitis, bubonic plague, staphylococcus, diphtheria, and typhoid.

In **1934, human trials** followed successful cancer cures in rats. Rife himself demanded that a research committee, comprised of physicians at the top of the most prestigious medical associations, had to be part of the proceedings. **At the end of 100 days, 16 terminally ill patients with various cancers were declared cured. The patients only required two 3-minute sessions per week to achieve total recovery.** Rife had determined that the lymphatic system needed time to eliminate the destroyed viruses, which dictated the limitation on how frequently the treatments could be made.

But this amazing information was buried by the American Medical Association under the influence of Dr. Morris Fishbein. It was this same campaign that vilified chiropractic treatments and doctors and anyone practicing energetic healing. It was a 50-year fight waged by the AMA whose work was threatened by actual healing modalities not based upon pharmaceuticals. In 1990 the U.S. Supreme Court upheld the 1987 trial finding the AMA and others guilty of an illegal conspiracy against the chiropractic profession.

Dr. Wilhelm Reich (1897-1957)

Dr. Wilhelm Reich is still noted historically for his work in psychiatry and psychoanalysis. However, Dr. Reich's work in biophysics has been stricken from the historical record. For at least a decade, the Federal Drug Administration, after putting Reich in prison, actively pursued a campaign to destroy all the books, notes, and research papers it could find containing the word "orgone". Judging by the government's actions, orgone energy is some kind of a threat and therefore must exist.

Well, what is orgone? Star Wars fans might call it "The Force", the Chinese "Chi", the Indians "Prana", and Polynesians "Mana". I have wondered if Christians would call it "The Holy Spirit". To Reich, it was "an etheric bio-energetic life force" that animates our environment and he called it "Orgone".

Reich's unique contribution was to determine that metal would attract an orgone energy flow through it, while anything organic attracted orgone and then stored it like a battery would store electric energy. He built Orgone Accumulators that were small boxes a patient could sit in. Reich used metal sheets to attract the orgone and then release it into organic material, like cotton or wood, that would surround the patient with beneficial, high doses of concentrated orgone energy. It is reported that some of his patients in advanced stages of cancer were cured. Faster healing, increased plant growth, and positive effects on overall health were also noted.

There are many types of energy healing devices, techniques, and modalities. The reason for only mentioning two is that they demonstrate the problem. Both Rife and Reich had devices reported to be capable of healing cancer with energy. Rife did not fight the establishment suggesting his studies be sidelined. Reich ignored the warnings, ending up with a prison sentence of two years, but Reich was dead in one year. Attempts to bury both theories were successful for a time. Now these theories are being cited as corroboration for current scientific discoveries, such as the one shown in the video on the magic frequency.

Why keep it secret?

Raymond Royal Rife, back in the 1930s, had accurately made the connection between energy fields in all biological life and the concept of sympathetic resonance. This is electromagnetic warfare inside a physical body. Find the vibration of your enemy, in this case a cancer cell, and cause it to start vibrating until it is destroyed.

Rife's contemporary was Nikola Tesla who was simultaneously also working on the concept of Resonance.

This excerpt is from https://blog.world-mysteries.com, January 11, 2016, titled: "Why did Tesla say that 3,6,9 was the key to the universe?"

> *Excerpt from the New York World Telegram, July 11, 1935*
>
> *Nikola Tesla revealed that an earthquake, which drew police and ambulances to the region of his laboratory at 48 E. Houston St., New York, in **1898**, was the result of a little machine he was experimenting with at the time which "you could put in your overcoat pocket." The bewildered newspapermen pounced upon this as at least one thing they*

could understand and Nikola Tesla, "the father of modern electricity" told what had happened as follows:

Tesla stated, "I was experimenting with vibrations. I had one of my machines going and I wanted to see if I could get it in tune with the vibration of the building. I put it up notch after notch. There was a peculiar cracking sound. I asked my assistants where did the sound come from. They did not know. I put the machine up a few more notches. There was a louder cracking sound. I knew I was approaching the vibration of the steel building. I pushed the machine a little higher. "Suddenly all the heavy machinery in the place was flying around. I grabbed a hammer and broke the machine. The building would have been about our ears in another few minutes. Outside in the street there was pandemonium. The police and ambulances arrived. I told my assistants to say nothing. We told the police it must have been an earthquake. That's all they ever knew about it."

Some shrewd reporter asked Dr. Tesla at this point what he would need to destroy the Empire State Building and the doctor replied: "Vibration will do anything. It would only be necessary to step up the vibrations of the machine to fit the natural vibration of the building and the building would come crashing down. That's why soldiers break step crossing a bridge."

https://blog.world-mysteries.com/science/why-did-tesla-say-that-369-was-the-key-to-the-universe/

Killing cancer cells without damaging surrounding cells would seem to be no threat to the establishment except for pharmaceutical/medical systems. If we are honest, they make money from sick people, not healthy people. But would money really be the reason for burying both Tesla's concepts (they were buried) and Rife's cancer healing technique, or were both concepts buried because they are the basis for very scary weapons? Tesla's theories could have taken down the Twin Towers on September 11, 2001, where the buildings just turned to dust. Rife's understanding of cellular response allows for the same sympathetic resonance be used against healthy cells, and those theories are behind directed energy weapons against biological targets.

But I digress. Maybe not. The fact that some very amazing discoveries, which would have made humanity's life experience so much less painful, have been buried and kept secret is just perplexing. Unless we look at the fact that the same science that can destroy a specific type of cell can also take down a building. Maybe those in power wanted to keep the information secret to keep our enemies from using it to make weapons. They wanted to bury the concept of Enerology.

And what about Dr. Wilhelm Reich and orgone? Can orgone be made into a weapon? Well, yes. In addition to his work of using orgone to heal, Reich also built the "Cloudbuster" to alter the weather.

Reich with Cloudbuster

A Reich cloudbuster can completely deactivate nuclear devices for great distances by drawing away the soft electron concentration from the vicinity of such a device. In fact a cloudbuster can be used for downing fleets of planes carrying nuclear weapons. Combustion is also dependent on soft electron concentrations which of course includes jet engines. Therefore jet engines or missiles cannot function in an area affected by a cloudbuster. For a mere several thousand dollar investment any country can be rendered invulnerable to any missile and nuclear weapon attack!...

It is evident that the proper use of the cloudbuster could throw modern warfare back to the Stone Age.... The cloudbuster or could even nullify this kind of hostilities obviously the drawing of soft particles away from any group would completely innervate each individual and even turn them into a

> *block of frozen flesh although a cloudbuster could not completely deactivate a particle beam weapon it could bring down any aircraft carrying such a device before it could get into position. -The Awesome Life Force by Joseph H. Cater, 1984, pg 253*

So it looks like those who prevented amazing healing techniques and devices from ever becoming commonplace were only trying to keep potential weapons secret. They were more interested in potential weapon technology than the health of their fellow humans. Rife was working in the 1930s about to erupt into the Second World War. Reich was working in the age of nuclear bombs and the Cold War.

But let's face it, when has there ever been a time when people were more important than weapons? As the Office Manager of a company making a piece of equipment that was no more than a handle, I witnessed the patent was held up for over 18 months. The very expensive patent attorney we paid informed us that the US Government was considering not giving us a patent as our patent could be essentially confiscated under the marking "State Security".

This policy of keeping innovative ideas as State Secrets has been ongoing since at least the 1930s; it intensified after nuclear bombs came on the scene, and finally was made into the 1952 Invention Secrecy Act, which allows patents considered "detrimental to the national security" to be on lockdown. So, yes, nothing is sacred if the Government wants to make it secret. And this is a law!

My point here is how many people have suffered and are suffering or will suffer from cancer when they do not have to? Just because you do not run your car on water does not mean it is not possible. Just because you cannot hook into "free energy" developed by Nikola Tesla and many others does not mean free energy does not exist. I could go on but I think you get my point.

And just because the concepts found in Enerology are not taught in US schools does not mean it is not understood. The Energy Universe is all around us and discussed in textbooks and ancient healing arts. We call the study of the energy universe "Enerology"; a new name for a vast source of knowledge spanning mankind's existence.

ENEROLOGY

The first premise of Enerology is that we live in an energy universe and the material 3D world, as depicted by contemporary science, is energy vibrating at the same basic rate resulting in the "frozen energy" of the material universe. You simply cannot have matter without an energy blueprint.

The second premise of enerology is that basic energy blueprints in the material universe are "Thought-Forms" manifested during conscious thinking. Nikola Tesla, the most prolific scientific mind of the modern era, would imagine complicated devices to the point that he could mentally see them operating and mentally fix any initial design flaws. Then Tesla would pull together the 3D pieces required to make his imagined device work in the material world.

The 300-plus patents owned by Tesla are the basis for virtually all the EM/WiFi devices and concepts propelling our technological society. None of this science existed until Tesla imagined it - thus creating a thought-form that was then transformed into such things as a radio or a system of

AC-electric powering everything. It all started with a thought that was imagining what could be.

Think of the riddle, "What came first, the chicken or the egg?" Disregarding the fact that the rooster "came first", it was not the chicken nor the egg it was the thought that brought them into existence. The question is, what was the thought?

Let's go with the simple, "I am hungry...and I need something to eat." Human thought is so powerful that the "Universe" began creating something to eat and a story to explain how it came about. Because the Universe is so endlessly resourceful, the story created both the chicken to eat and, to make sure you are kept in food, the egg. And, of course, the rooster was critical to the story so creation manifested something that is not particularly tasty but needed nonetheless within 3D reality.

This concept of thought dictating the construct of any given reality is at the very core of Quantum Physics. It is also why Quantum Physics has not been universally embraced by many scientific disciplines and scientists. Quantum physicists concluded very early in their studies and experiments, conducted at the atomic and subatomic levels, that whatever the researcher thought would happen was exactly what did happen. And they proved it in many ways and in many experiments. At the very smallest observable level of our 3D reality thought controls what happens.

Max Planck, the originator of Quantum theory, put it this way, "*I regard consciousness as fundamental. I regard matter as derivative from consciousness. We cannot get behind consciousness. Everything that we talk about, everything that we regard as existing, postulates consciousness."*

So, ok... but where is all this energy coming from that can meld itself into material 3D manifestation following an energetic blue print of a thought?

The Quantum Field as defined within enerology is the place where "Proto-Energy" resides. Proto-energy can be seen as waves or particles of pure energy that are the building blocks of all 3D manifestations. All that ever was, is or will be, begins as proto-energy in the Quantum Field. The key to manifestation is to access the Quantum Field and the proto-energy.

In my opinion, the most important principle of quantum physics is that to have manifestation you must have a conscious thought behind it. This quirky and bothersome concept was one of the first astounding observations of the quantum or molecular world. It has come to be called the "observer effect". When scientists were able to observe the smallest particles in the physical world, their experiments concluded that whatever they thought would happen happened.

As physicist Pascual Jordan noted, "...observations not only disturb what has to be measured, they produce it... We compel [a quantum particle] to assume a definite position." Jordan also said, "...we ourselves produce the results of measurements."

According to contemporary theory in physics, the Quantum Field contains an infinite amount of energy. If we assume that energy can be called into 3D existence by creative thought, it stands to reason we also have infinite potential for creation that is only limited by creative consciousness.

Well, this is where Shungite comes into the discussion. In studying the properties of Shungite, we began witnessing what happens when a finite object (Shungite) can access infinite power within the Quantum Field. The key to Shungite's magic is it does access the Quantum Field, and the key to our understanding of the Quantum Field is Shungite.

What Walt Silva and I brought to the table was looking at Shungite from the concept of enerology. Others focused on the materialistic approach, deciding that the secret to Shungite's healing attributes was the antioxidants that seemed to be produced in the water. They decided that to get the healing and the water detoxification effects of Shungite water, you had to use a pile of it and replace it regularly. If radiation confronts Shungite shielding then the negation of the radioactivity must be due to Shungite blocking or absorbing the radiation. The same thing with EM/WiFi signals being blocked or absorbed by Shungite.

SHUNGITE SCIENCE

Walt Silva

In September 2014, Walt Silva was given an audio podcast where I was explaining what I knew about Shungite at that time. He had already heard about Shungite and actually had nuggets that he did not know what to do with until he heard my theories. He immediately began experimenting.

Walt's childhood and most of his teenage years were spent in Argentina. As an only child with a father who brought books into the home on subjects outside the norm, Walt was introduced to esoteric thought and thinking outside the box. It did not take him long to realize that continuing his education within the established system of higher education would take away his creativity and firmly imprison him inside a box. It is a box where everyone believes the same... if you want to be successful.

My interpretation is that Walt, like so many others, found a way of making money by embracing computer technology and becoming a very knowledgeable computer technician. But his life was focused on the invisible side of existence where energy rules. He not only studied Raymond Rife and Wilhelm Reich, he duplicated and experimented with some of their devices. Walt followed this with current research into the world of energy being done by Don Croft and Slim Spurling. By the time Walt met me, he had built and experimented with a variety of devices including those pursuing orgone energy.

Orgone Energy

Most scientists would say orgone is a figment of the imagination, as it is technically not measurable with any currently known meter. Proof of orgone's existence is in the results of its supposed use and in the testimonials of people who can actually sense, by feelings and sight, orgone and other energies such as electrical or electronic fields. And, Wilhelm Reich apparently did create a way to visualize and photograph orgone. Today we also have photographic proof of its existence.

Supposedly, orgone will become visible enough to photograph if it is within an electromagnetic field. On the moon, with their spacesuits emitting radio frequencies to communicate and other monitoring devices, astronauts appear to have excited the naturally occurring orgone on the moon (even in a vacuum). There is a photograph of an astronaut surrounded by a blue cloud. The light glow in this rendition is actually blue in the color photograph.

In one situation, psychics who could see energies provided guidance by being able to describe the form, movements, and color of energies associated with a given orgone device. Walt wished he could also have someone who could explain the energies he was creating with his orgone devices.

BOOM! Walt had formulated a thought getting the attention of that Spiritual Intervention mechanism. Walt wanted someone who could see energies. As cited previously in this book, I am energy sensitive. I can also either imagine or actually perceive energies, molecules, atoms and the doorway to the Quantum Field. When I began working with Shungite and seeing its amazing energetic properties, I asked the USI for someone who could take what was in my head and make it real. So someone sent Walt a podcast and we both got what we had asked for.

I would explain to Walt what I was seeing and he would create an experiment to test my observations. If he confirmed what I was saying, we would discuss the implications of it. In the first chapter, I cover how this ended up in products that make better use of Shungite. We will now take a look at the enerology side of the journey where science and metaphysics come together.

1. Shungite accelerates both electric signals and the flow of orgone.

Whatever Walt heard me say on the podcast led him to a test regarding the flow of electricity. Using an ohm meter, Walt confirmed that Shungite nuggets conduct electricity measurable as a fraction of an ohm up to 3 ohms.

Then he decided to see what would happen if he added Shungite to an orgone device called an implosion coil. Walt determined the orgone flowing through the coil of copper was moving four times faster, in addition, the orgone spiral device actually had a drop in temperature measured as a 1 degree Celsius drop.

Seeing the effects that Shungite had on orgone, Walt devised another experiment, but this time to test how Shungite affects electricity.

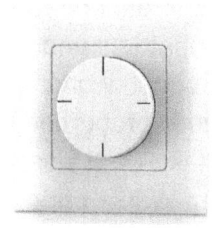

A dimmer switch turns down the amount of electricity running into the light or fan to control brightness or speed. Four marks were added to the dimmer and measurements were taken of how much electricity was running through the switch at each of the four marks.

With the dimmer controlling the amount of electricity flowing to a fan, Walt could determine if the speed of the electricity was changed by adding a Shungite nugget to the circuit. Actually, two nuggets were added because there were two wires connecting the fan to the electric system. There is a wire carrying the power and a wire to complete the circuit called the neutral wire. Walt cut both wires and spliced each wire back into the circuit, but between the two cut ends he added a Shungite nugget.

What Walt observed was that at each of the four points on the dimmer, his original readings were lower. While very small, there was a measurable increase of milliamps flowing through the system. Shungite had accelerated the flow of electricity, but why?

He and I had a conversation and posed the concept that perhaps the fact that orgone moved faster within a Shungite field could answer an age-old question. Why was there resistance to the flow of electricity through a wire? Walt's experience with orgone, following Wilhelm Reich's observations of the way orgone was attracted to and flowed through metal, made him suspect it was orgone simultaneously moving through the wire at a slower speed than electricity that was causing resistance. If Shungite accelerated orgone simultaneously flowing through the same wire being used for electricity, and orgone was what caused resistance, the electricity would encounter less resistance and flow faster.

Whatever this Shungite was, it was powerful. Either it could directly affect orgone and therefore the flow of electricity, or it was somehow directly affecting simultaneously both orgone and electricity causing the signals to move faster.

2. Shungite reverses electric and radio waves.

Working with a few other energy sensitive individuals, we identified that 15 grams of Shungite nuggets were enough to cause the rotation of energy fields emanating from an electric system to reverse spin. The energy coming off the electric system in a home is rotating opposite to the rotation of a human cell. This causes friction, seen as a buildup of heat, and a degrading of the cell itself. With just 15 grams of Shungite nuggets, the change in rotation resulted in an energy field that, while still unnatural, was at least biocompatible.

It was not surprising that the apparent detrimental health effects of EM/WiFi/radio/radiation signals were because the signals were rotating opposite to biological cells. Our cells rotate one way and these unnatural frequencies rotate in the opposite direction. Walt realized that the spin of the signal, which was detrimental to health, was caused by the way they created the fundamentals of electric motor technology.

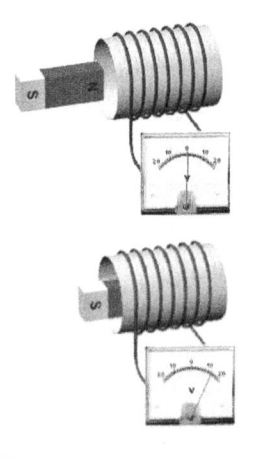

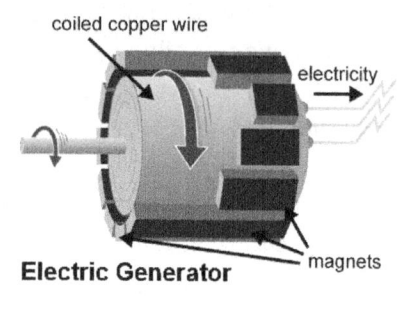

Electric Generator

Michael Faraday's electric magnetic rotation apparatus (motor)

In 1830, British scientist Michael Faraday discovered that he could create an electric current by moving magnets inside coils of copper wire. This is still the first step in creating electricity even in today's power plants. It is where the problem began.

Since the beginning, there has been an accepted direction for the copper wire to be wrapped. The direction of wrapping dictates the direction that the created electric signal rotates. Unfortunately that rotation is contrary to biological life. However, Shungite's powerful energy field can cause the electric signals to reverse rotation.

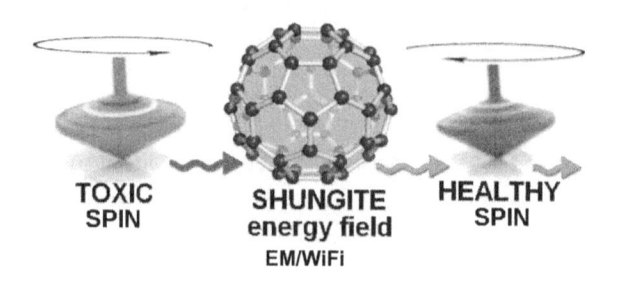

TOXIC SPIN — SHUNGITE energy field EM/WiFi — HEALTHY SPIN

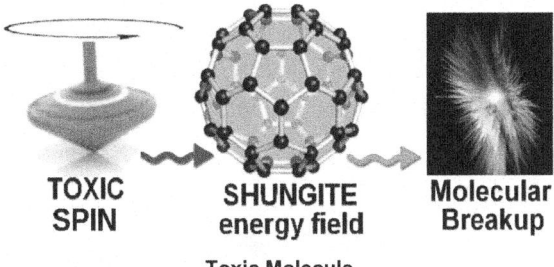

| TOXIC SPIN | SHUNGITE energy field | Molecular Breakup |

Toxic Molecule

3. Any molecule toxic to biological life is rotating opposite to the way our cells rotate and Shungite can reverse its spin causing a loss of molecular cohesion.

Walt had also determined that anything toxic to biological life is rotating opposite to the way our cells rotate. If Shungite puts out an energy field powerful enough to cause electric signals to reverse their spin, was the field strong enough to cause molecules to reverse their spin? The answer is yes.

For centuries, the ability of Shungite to purify water has been known. Water purifying systems have replaced the carbon with Shungite. Water comes into the purifier and is filtered through carbon or Shungite. In the case of carbon, it has to be replaced often, as it absorbs toxic particles from the water and the carbon becomes a toxic sponge.

In two identified Russian studies, testing was done to determine how long before the Shungite should be replaced, because it would be more polluted than the water, as was the case with carbon. Much to their surprise, they discovered there was no toxic buildup in Shungite. The water was definitely purified but the toxins had just disappeared. The only explanation is this: the molecules entered the Shungite energy field and were forced to reverse their energy spin. But unlike electricity that is pure energy, these were molecules comprised of atoms. As the reversal of the spin begins, the molecular cohesion keeping all the atoms energetically connected is disrupted and the atoms just break away, leaving only scattered atoms and no toxic molecules.

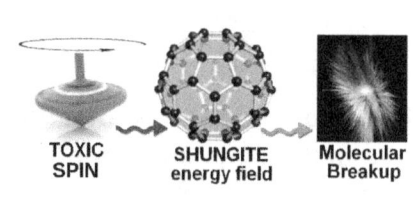

Wow! We now had a scientific reason why Shungite is the world's best water purifier. It never has to be replaced except for the eventual wear down of the Shungite particles themselves. Shungite is not a super-hard material and rubbing or running water through it will very slowly wear down the size of the Shungite granules.

TOXIC SPIN — SHUNGITE energy field — Molecular Breakup

4. Secondary electric devices need Shungite to attenuate their electric fields.

We assumed that when the **electric system in the house** was attenuated, all the electric devices would be putting out energy fields that were biocompatible. We discovered this was not true. As mentioned above, the real problem with the system is the way the first electric generators were wired. The wiring dictates which way the field rotates. If the wiring had been reversed, the energy field would have already been biocompatible and we would not be in the situation we are in now. **With every secondary motor** you have such as a hairdryer, washing machine, electric stove and any other electrical device, the resulting energy field is in a toxic rotation. Thankfully, by the time we realized this, we had already discovered the power of Shungite powder.

5. A nugget of Shungite is more energetic than a large rock of Shungite.

In fact, Shungite powder is really the most energetic form of Shungite. I am saying it is more energetic, not more powerful. The concept of power is not in play when talking about Shungite. This particular observation led to our creation of stickers. It was a much more convenient way of providing a more energetic Shungite field to an electric system. We called this the Bucky Bandaid sticker.

Without a doubt, just Raw Shungite powder on a typical label attached to anything with an electric motor will attenuate the electric signal. An "electric device" is something that <u>does</u> something. Your washing machine, air/heating units, refrigerators etc., are all electric devices with a secondary motor. An electric clock is an electric device that does not have a secondary motor and the signal from your electric system, if already attenuated, will make the clock biologically compatible.

"Electronic devices" communicate in some way, and while the Bucky Bandaid Sticker did attenuate most electronic emissions, it was not completely successful when dealing with WiFi. When placed on the cell phone, there was a change but I could still detect negatively rotating energy fields associated with the cell phone.

I have to make a note here. One of the key elements behind the concept of enerology is you have to ask the right question to get the right answer. The question I was asking at this point was, what else is needed to attenuate the cell phone signal?

6. Silver Saturated Shungite attenuates WiFi signals.

Shungite makes a connection to the Quantum Field and the proto-energy flows into Shungite's natural energy field that provides the power to spin the field at over 20 billion times a second. I saw this energetically. But initially we could not identify what was causing the amazing connection..

At this point in the game I had been focusing on energy fields. I could actually see and feel shifts in energy. As we worked with each different version of a product, I would look at it and feel it to make some observation. In the case of a raw nugget being wrapped in wire, I could virtually see the energy field coming off the wire as I was wrapping it around the nugget.

It was the wire that gave me the next big insight into Shungite. The first pendants that I had wrapped used a silver coated copper wire. I was talking to a friend of mine wearing one of those originals and I suddenly realized I was no longer seeing silver on the wire, I was seeing the copper. Where did the silver go? It was not scratched off, it was uniformly just gone.

I told Walt what had happened and he said something to the effect that silver migrates. This migration of silver was noted when silver solder is used in electronics. After a time, the nanoparticles of silver actually leave the solder. This is why gold is much more preferred when working with electronics.

So then Walt took some nuggets and threw them in a solution of colloidal silver that contained microscopic flakes of pure silver. A few hours later the solution was clear and the silver was now contained in the Shungite nuggets. The silver had become impregnated into the Shungite. Walt attempted scraping the Shungite to see if the silver coating was just on the outside, but nothing happened. Walt sent me these nuggets and an entirely new view of what was happening with Shungite emerged.

I called the new nuggets "Silver Saturated Shungite". As I focused on the nugget, instead of stopping at the energy field, I was drawn deeper to a point where I could observe the following. At the Quantum Level of energy the Shungite appeared to be connected to a vortex or energy door. It was the door to the Quantum Field where the proto-energy of all that is, was, and will be is contained. The third dimensional reality we think of as being the universe is probably less than 10% of all that is and the rest is within the Quantum Field.

I took a raw Shungite nugget and also focused at the quantum level. I saw the doorway but there was a difference. In looking at the raw Shungite, the doorway to the Quantum Field was pulsing. It was like a door that was opening and closing. But the Silver Saturated Shungite had the door opened with no pulsing. The result was that the silver-saturated nugget was drawing a continuous field of quantum energy into the third dimension.

I got the cell phone that already had a Bucky Bandaid and focused on the energy signature coming off the phone. Then I placed one of the Silver Saturated Shungite nuggets on top of the phone. I immediately felt and could see a drastic change in the signature. What I had been missing is the complexity of the cell phone field, including it being a square wave instead of the sine wave associated with simple electric energies.

The Bucky Bandaid by itself, with just the raw Powder pulsing, was not enough to attenuate the square wave of the cell phone signal, but with the silver added and the quantum door open all the time, the stream of quantum energy was able to attenuate the square wave. With just the raw Shungite, the field would hit the wave, stop, and the wave would bounce back. With the silver keeping the door to the Quantum Field open, square waves attenuated easily. The WiFi energy field had no time to bounce back.

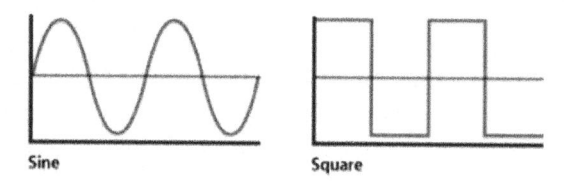

Sine   Square

By making a mix of Raw Shungite and the Silver Saturated Shungite and putting it on a label, Walt Silva had created the Silver Saturated Shungite Sticker, commonly called the S4 Sticker. These are what you should use to attenuate WiFi signals. The mix of powders we used in the Stickers soon made their way into resin. By wearing an S4 Resin Pendant, WiFi signals are made biocompatible before the signal actually hits you.

7. The Buckyball C60 Fullerene is the secret behind Shungite.

We were seeing how Shungite was working and how to work with the different versions of it. We were even able to see the quantum connection. But what was making this connection to the Quantum Field door? It was a carbon molecule, discovered in a lab in 1985. The 1996 Nobel Prize in Chemistry was awarded for the discovery of a new molecule called the fullerene to:

- Professor Robert F. Curl, Jr., Rice University, Houston, USA,

- Professor Sir Harold W. Kroto, University of Sussex, Brighton, U.K., and

- Professor Richard E. Smalley, Rice University, Houston, USA,

> New forms of the element carbon – called fullerenes – in which the atoms are arranged in closed shells was discovered in 1985 by Robert F. Curl, Harold W. Kroto and Richard E. Smalley. The number of carbon atoms in the shell can vary, and for this reason numerous new carbon structures have become known. Formerly, six crystalline forms of the element carbon were known, namely two kinds of graphite, two kinds of diamond, chaoit and carbon(VI). The latter two were discovered in 1968 and 1972

- The Royal Swedish Academy of Sciences, 10/9/1996 Press Release

This new molecule called the C60 fullerene, created in a laboratory, has gone on to be one of the most investigated molecules in history. It is a very large molecule rotating billions of times a second and has been investigated by many different modalities of science. A Google search returned 1,090,000 results for the term "C60 fullerene" (8/30/2019).

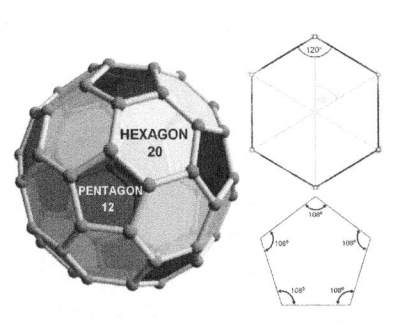

There are 120 symmetry operations,

like rotations around an axis or reflections in a plane, which map the molecule onto itself. This makes C60 the molecule with the largest number of symmetry operations or the most symmetric molecule known. Chemistry alone has embraced a new branch called Fullerene-Chemistry.

The C60 Fullerene is a molecule comprised of 60 carbon atoms. The pattern the atoms take has resulted in a new category of carbon molecules. Unlike other carbon-based graphite or diamond patterns that are created in a flat plane, the fullerene atomic pattern actually creates complicated geometric shapes that allow them to have an interior. In other words they create hollow shapes or shells and the most perfect shape is the C60, which looks like an American soccer ball.

The story goes that the new carbon molecules, known as "fullerenes", were named after Buckminster Fuller, who promoted the use of geodesic domes for construction as they are architecturally stronger than other geometric shapes. The C60 itself is nicknamed the Buckyball and is reminiscent of two geodesic domes with their bases together.

I suspect this is not the real reason behind these rather magical molecules being named to honor Buckminster Fuller. Fuller is best known for his thoughts on architecture. But Fuller is equally famous in scientific circles for his work on "The Vector Equilibrium".

"The Vector Equilibrium"

In its most basic definition, vector equilibrium occurs when a geometric shape has equal lines and equal angles. When energy is introduced to the shape, the energy follows the geometry. At a certain point "...the movement of energy comes to a state of absolute equilibrium, and therefore absolute stillness and nothingness." As Fuller states, "because of this it is the zero-phase from which all other forms emerge." (http://cosmometry.net/vector-equilibrium-&-isotropic-vector-matrix)

Fuller himself put it this way: "The Vector Equilibrium is the zero starting point for happenings or non-happenings: it is the empty theater and empty circus and empty universe ready to accommodate any act and any audience." – Cite Synergetic's (2nd. Ed.) at Sec. 503.03; 11 Dec '75.

As mentioned earlier in this book, Russian scientist, Dr. Semeon J. Tsirpursky, had been working on carbon atoms found in Shungite before going to Arizona State University, where he saw an electron micrograph image of synthetic C60. He realized this same molecule had been identified in Shungite.

Shungite was analyzed by a mass spectrometer that found it contained both the C60 and the C70 fullerenes. C70 has 70 atoms and the shell looks more like an American football. These fullerene molecules are contained within the carbon content of Shungite and that varies depending upon where the sample came from within the Shungite field.

After hearing about the C60 molecule I made the Shungite C60 connection. I came to understand vector equilibrium and was wowed by Buckminster Fuller's claim that "The Vector Equilibrium is the zero starting point for happenings or non-happenings...." The C60 had the largest number of symmetry operations. As the most symmetric molecule yet discovered the C60 is likely the biggest empty theater in the universe.

The C60 takes vector equilibrium to a new level. Vector equilibrium with its equal angles and distances between the 60 carbon atoms creates multiple zero points that open the door to the Quantum Field, in a way no other identified molecular structure can. We had begun to state that Shungite accessed infinite power in a finite object. Now I had a scientific explanation as to why that was true.

But there was a problem. Knowing what to look for, I looked for the C60 molecule in Shungite. Much to my surprise, I found them but very few of them. While I did not advertise this observation, I did begin telling people that you only needed one C60 to create the Shungite magic. To give you an idea of what I saw, in a typical nugget wrapped in wire as a pendant you might only find 3 to 6 of the C60 molecules, and honestly in some nuggets there was no C60.

However, a nugget without a C60 molecule energetically reacts as if it had a bunch of C60 molecules. It comes down to the quantum entanglement concept so perplexing that Einstein observed it was "spooky action at a distance."

8. Each particle of Shungite has a quantum entanglement with the Mother Lode in Karelia.

An article posted on sciencealert.com by Fiona Macdonald (13 July 2019) is titled: "Scientists Just Unveiled The First-Ever Photo of Quantum Entanglement."

Quantum entanglement is a term given when two particles become inextricably linked, and whatever happens to one immediately affects the other, regardless of how far apart they are. Quantum scientists looking at material particles have observed that pairs or even groups of particles can be linked at the quantum level even when the particles are separated by large distances.

In the case of Shungite, there is a quantum entanglement between each particle of Shungite and the Mother Lode in Karelia. The connection is very much one of energy and incorporates vibration and resonance to link every piece of Shungite to every other piece of Shungite via the Mother Lode.

While we do not have access to the expensive equipment quantum scientists use to venture into the quantum field, we do have energy-sensitive people who may be the best observers. After five and a half years of working with Shungite, I have seen it change as more people began working with it. Shungite keeps getting more cohesive and every version becomes more energetic. In the beginning, I was not impressed with geometric shapes and beads compared with raw specimens. But today even the machined Shungite is equivalent to a good quality Raw nugget.

Quantum Entanglement

Let's take a deeper look at quantum entanglement from the standpoint of energetic signatures and sympathetic resonance. Each individual human has a unique energy signature. But while each individual is completely unique, there are many factors making up the individual's signature that can be duplicated in many other individuals.

DNA plays a critical role, and anyone with a similar DNA signature maintains a similar energy signature. A family vibrates and resonates in a similar signature. When it comes to identical twins, the signatures are virtually identical genetically and only their life experiences set them apart in their unique energy signatures.

Beyond family units, there are similar signatures in individuals coming from the same culture and same area of the world. Locations have frequencies and every frequency can be affected by other frequencies. The closer the frequency signatures, the more resonance is created. People coming from the same location pick up subtle energy imprints from that location. They will have a quantum entanglement.

As far as culture is concerned, there is also a quantum entanglement that springs from common beliefs and traditional stories. As an example, for Americans the story of Bambi. Actually, the name of the book is *Bambi, a Life in the Woods* by Austrian author Felix Salten. It was the basis for the 1942 Walt Disney movie simply called "Bambi". Every child who read, or especially watched, the story was forever linked energetically, if they had that "aha moment" of understanding that death creates grief and fear.

What the %$#@ were the parents thinking? Children do not need to confront this information as a night-time story or a Disney movie! Yes, life will eventually teach the lesson, but when presented to children through one extraordinary story, a quantum connection is made. Every society has a library of stories presented to every individual in the society, forever etching a specific set of energy parameters into each individual's energy field. Another quantum connection.

People's shared religions, political beliefs, occupations, experiences and even the groups they hang out with as friends - even on Facebook - all add a specific energy parameter to their own unique energy signature. In Enerology, a parameter is a set of energies that defines specific genetics, locations, experiences, and associations that are, in fact, shared with millions of other people. The more of these parameters you share with someone the more sympathetic resonance occurs.

It may just be that in an energy universe the quantum entanglements are the glue holding it all together. It may also be that sympathetic resonance is what keeps everything moving and alive.

Let's take a look at the landscape of Nature; and this I learned as metaphysical thought. For every tree species, like an oak, pine, redwood, etc., there is an energetic weave connecting them. For every type of mineral, like ruby, emerald, quartz, etc., there is also a weave of connecting energy. And there is another connection between all the trees and also between all the minerals. Shungite has an energetic weave connecting every particle that came out of the Karelian deposit to every other particle. All of these examples are quantum entanglement.

Each mineral has a unique energy signature based upon molecular and chemical composition. It is rather like a genetic parameter in the Animal Kingdom. For the vast majority of minerals, a secondary parameter is where they were created - the location parameter. In the case of Shungite, it can only be mined from one deposit in Karelia.

But Shungite was not created in Karelia. Some claim that Shungite evolved from the decayed remains of the very first life forms that started growing on Earth. But how can this be true when Shungite has fullerene molecules? To be specific, on Earth, the $C60$ molecule can be found in soot remaining from a fire; in areas where there has been a meteorite strike; and in an area hit by lightning. In 2019, the Hubble Space Telescope detected the large and complex ionized molecules of $C60$ in the interstellar medium between the stars. Super high heat is not part of the process of decay from plant into mineral. But with Shungite being created in interstellar space, the $C60$ would virtually be a required ingredient, as it appears to be a very popular cosmic molecule.

Shungite was created in outer space. It was infused with cosmic energies all along its journey to Karelia. There are cosmic energy parameters integral to the makeup of the mineral composite we know of as Shungite. Every particle of Shungite is forever linked energetically to every other particle.

9. Shungite C60 is superior to Lab made C60.

Technically, Shungite and lab made C60 are the same. 60 atoms of carbon follow the same pattern to make the C60 molecule. Personally, I have never met a lab-made C60 I resonated with. Why?

I suspect the C60 molecules, and carbon atoms in general, have an affinity for picking up and storing both biologically created and cosmic energies. Shungite was created in an environment of cosmic interstellar energies and that is the dominating parameter in the Shungite energy signature.

Lab-made C60 also picks up energies, but I would not call them cosmic. The dominating energy parameter in lab C60 is different in products manufactured by different companies. The C60 picks up the energies surrounding it while it is being created and processed. Some of those energies emanate from whatever the C60 is mixed with. Water has a different signature than olive oil, and every version of either water or oil has its own specific energy signature.

And let us not forget about the human thought pervading the environment of the lab. Do you suppose the cosmic Shungite C60 is carrying small energy parameters of thought from people who are frustrated, tired, mentally and physically unhealthy, hateful, envious, jealous, fearful, etcetera? Well, lab C60 is full of it, and that is why I would not get near it with a ten-foot pole.

Ah, but you counter, does it also pick up energies of love, appreciation, gratitude, and joy emitted as human emotion and thought? Well yes it does. And wouldn't that be wonderful if that was the predominant environment of the typical workplace? How many of you work in a love-filled environment?

This concept of quantum entanglement was well understood by myself and Walt and then by Derek and Maureen Condit. We realized that every piece of Shungite that came through us would leave carrying an energy parameter called "Cosmic Reality". We have diligently worked at keeping that energy signature one of love, appreciation, gratitude, and joy.

10. Shungite loves energy fields.

Shungite loves all energy fields and that includes human-generated fields such as thoughts and emotions.

Walt's initial interactions with Shungite showed it enhanced the flow of both orgone and electricity. When the S4 powder resin had a magnet added to it, it was determined that Shungite also took magnetism to a new level.

Initially the magnets were added to the S4 Resin Pendant mold. After the resin cured, Walt drilled holes at both ends and sent it to me. I took the new S4 magnet and made a beaded Shungite bracelet incorporating the S4 magnet. I knew about the benefits of magnets and wanted to see what the S4 magnet would do for the physical body. I have not taken it off in about four years. However, we do not sell these bracelets for many reasons, mostly because you do not need them if you are wearing a pendant.

Walt's mom noted that the S4 magnets would also make a great refrigerator magnet. As soon as Walt related this observation, I stuck an S4 Magnet on the refrigerator and felt the power of Shungite merging with other energy fields. What happened was an expansion, enhancement, and essentially an increase in the force of the energy field associated with the refrigerator.

The electric energy is powering the refrigerator. Orgone energy is being attracted by the metal frame of the refrigerator and accumulates in and around the metal frame. The Shungite has its own energy field being powered by the Quantum Field. Adding the magnetic field, even as small as it is, sets up a pattern of movement that creates a dynamic torsion field. A torsion field is a donut-shaped field of energy and an extremely common form of energy. In fact, the human bioelectromagnetic energy field is in the shape of a torsion field.

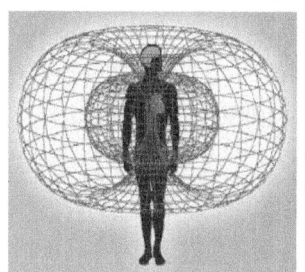

We also find torsion fields in pyramids. In the 3D reality, energy follows geometry. The unique geometric structure of a pyramid in and of itself creates a torsion field inside the structure. It is the torsion field that is behind the seemingly magical properties of a pyramid.

One pyramid researcher, Alexander Golod, who has been examining pyramids since 1990 in Russia, observed that pyramids have the power to eliminate viruses and even treat cancer, preserve foods, intensify the potency of drugs, and many other surprises. Golod has led many studies on the effects of pyramids in different environments and situations. One study demonstrated that pyramids have agricultural effects, purportedly increasing the yield by 30 to 100 percent. Using military radar units, massive amounts of ionizing radiation was measured coming from the tips of the pyramids.

The torsion field found in a pyramid extends from the top to the bottom. A torsion field in a square (or a rectangle, like a refrigerator) will eventually situate itself in the top 15% of the square – like near the ceiling of a room. The torsion field created by the orgone, electric, magnetic, Shungite, and quantum fields retains a dynamic and self-perpetuating motion that permeates the entire refrigerator. It is contained within the refrigerator and surrounds the refrigerator, radiating many feet into the environment.

It was the dynamic torsion field bleeding into the environment that I had felt when I added the S4 Shungite Magnet. Shungite had just taught me something else. Whereas you can attenuate a signal to make it biocompatible, the signal still exists. It is a force of energy that is not natural, whether being radiated by the electric system or by electronic devices.

When merged with the Shungite field, these unnatural energy signals act as fuel to intensify the Shungite field. By putting a Shungite magnet on the refrigerator, the refrigerator becomes an energy device and the source of a very healing Shungite - orgone – electric – magnetic – quantum energy field radiating into the kitchen and surrounding rooms. And because you do not have to recharge or clean the Shungite magnet, that healing energy is always present.

Walt is fond of saying, "Shungite has not met a positive energy field it did not like." One of the documented observations of what happens when Shungite is added to an energy field is the continually reported electric cost savings achieved with the use of the magnets.

11. Shungite creates energy savings.

In 2016 we did a test at a restaurant by putting an S4 Shungite Magnet on each of three walk-in refrigerators and two large air-conditioners. After five months a comparison was made of electric bills from 2015, which averaged above $3,000 per month. The total saving over those five months was $4,803. (See CosmicReality.net and search "Shungite & Electric Savings".)

Walt has tested this observation by using an electric tool that could have its load accurately measured. The load is how much power is being put out and Walt measured it without, and then with one, two, and three Shungite Stickers. These were the Bucky Bandaids used with any device that has no WiFi. One sticker reduced the electricity needed to obtain the same load by 20%. A second sticker caused another decrease, and a third took the total power savings to 30%. Additional stickers made no difference. Why?

12. Three pieces of Shungite creates a coherent field.

Nicola Tesla said, "If you knew the magnificence of the three, six and nine, you would have a key to the universe." He also said, "If you want to find the secrets of the universe, think in terms of energy, frequency and vibration."

There are many who have tried to explain the meaning of these quotes. Honestly, most of them I cannot follow. But explaining Tesla is not my job. My goal is to present my observations, which appear to be confirmed by Tesla. There is something magical about three.

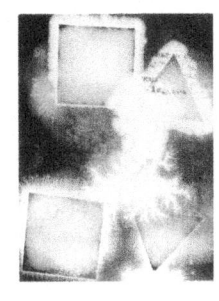

We knew that three nuggets and three stickers appeared to energetically connect with each other. And when you have three units of three, there is another connection between each of the units. Confirmation of the secondary field emerging from three pieces of Shungite came in the form of a Kirlian photograph taken by Sofiya Blank. Sofiya is a Russian scientist who has worked with both Walt and myself on the mission of understanding Shungite. Kirlian photography is a process that photographs energy fields. To Sofiya Blank we are deeply grateful.

From the beginning, we were aware that each nugget and, in fact, every particle of powder has a unique signature beyond the base Shungite energy. When any three nuggets or particles get within range of each other their fields create a secondary field that is "coherent" or has added stability. The Kirlian photograph of geometric shaped Shungite pieces demonstrates that secondary field. You can see the individual fields and an additional field linking the three pieces of Shungite together.

When all three sets of three connect, Tesla's formula of 3-6-9 being the key to understanding the universe is demonstrated. The best way I can phrase it is: three sets of three nuggets connecting on so many levels with the Quantum Field creates a complex but very stable field that links up with "Hyperspace". And what is Hyperspace? When I get that figured out I will report back.

13. Shungite promotes healing.

I saw the stunning improvement in my dog Josie's health with just the addition of a Shungite pendant, brought to me by Rev. Lee Brown in March 2014. There were a few Shungite websites discussing the health benefits of Shungite and the Russians were calling it "The Medicine of the 21st Century."

Over the next few months, various dogs and cats were given Shungite wrapped pendants and nuggets for their water. These were the first testimonials to the health benefits directly attributable to Shungite. There were obvious and sometimes stunning beneficial changes in the animals, and unlike humans who were also reporting positive results, animals are not known to listen to the radio or read! No placebo effect here.

Just a note on the placebo effect. In a 2012 Psychology Today article entitled "The Placebo Effect: How It Works" by Faith Brynie Ph.D., she states, "Estimates of the placebo cure rate range from a low of 15 percent to a high of 72 percent. The longer the period of treatment and the larger the number of physician visits, the greater the placebo." Before a pharmaceutical drug can be sold, it has to go through a placebo test. If up to 72% of people taking a sugar tablet instead of the drug has beneficial results, why has it taken so long for someone to throw away the pharmaceuticals and explore the concept that the mind alone can cure? Just asking.

Back to Shungite and the animals who had different ailments. What was it in the Shungite that created an energy field that seemingly could help with such a wide variety of ailments? It is reported that the Shungite field in Karelia has traces of every element in the periodic chart of elements. If this is true, and it does seem likely, Shungite is likely carrying every energy for every ailment. The periodic chart of elements is the list of molecules that comprise physical reality.

If we were right, the reason the waters in and around the Shungite deposit are observed to be healing is they are charged with every energy needed to heal the 3D body. It is the etheric and other energy bodies drawing on Shungite's huge inventory of energies that allows stabilization of those energy bodies. With the energy bodies healthy, healing of the physical body is possible. Shungite appears to posses all the energies we need to remain healthy. If not the complete answer, this has to be a partial answer as to why Shungite has a history of healing, especially in the lakes and waterways in the area of the Shungite field.

My main focus regarding Shungite was on the dangers of electromagnetic and WiFi radiation and what Shungite could do to make it not damaging. My first introduction to Shungite was a simple ring with a piece of Shungite in it, placed over the antenna of the Wi-Fi transmitter to completely transform that energy field from one that was very uncomfortable to one that was very soothing. For the first time in 40 years I saw the glimmer of hope.

All biological life on the planet is designed to operate in the unique energy field of an earth before the time of Thomas Edison and Nicola Tesla. Today, everything and everyone is continually confronted by man-made energy fields ranging from the coffee maker to power lines carrying instantaneous death, from the television to the computer, from microwave stations carrying telephone calls to radar systems guiding airplanes. They have a name for it now, they call it "electronic smog". And electronic smog is continually attacking the natural bioelectromagnetic field that equates to Life.

The United States Government's recommended standard for electric and radio emissions is 1,000 times higher than the mandatory standards set by Russia and other countries, and 1,000 times higher than the point at which DNA is changed. This has been true since I was first alerted to the dangers of these emissions.

In summary, even minor electromagnetic fields can cause such things as high blood pressure, insomnia, headaches, dizziness, nervousness, blood diseases, heart attacks, sexual disturbances, and birth defects. Raymond Rife demonstrated how EM signals can destroy a cancer cell through the concept of sympathetic resonance. The same mechanism is in play when encountering EM/WiFi signals. Instead of cancer cells being targeted, the effected cells are ALL cells!

Let's remind ourselves of what sympathetic resonance is. If you were to open a piano allowing the strings to be seen, an interesting phenomenon happens whenever you hit a given note. If, for instance, you hit Middle C, all other corresponding C strings begin to vibrate in unison. While these additional vibrations are not loud enough to be heard, the strings can be seen to vibrate. This is called "sympathetic resonance", a phenomenon seen throughout nature. For instance, the eardrum vibrates when encountering a sound wave, and 69-79% of sounds heard in the ear also resonate throughout the entire skeletal system.

Russian, European, and American scientists have found an alarming disturbance in brain waves, endocrine systems, and even reproductive functions resulting from low levels of electromagnetic impulses creating biological resonance within the physical cells. While high levels of radiation can rip atoms apart, low levels create cellular agitation - or imbalances. This imbalance has been demonstrated to actually reverse the natural spin of human blood in people suffering from electromagnetic pollution. It is interesting to note, in light of the growing proliferation of cancer, that cancer patients also have blood spinning in a reverse direction to those of healthy individuals.

In 1974, among other duties, I was the Safety Officer for my unit. I attended a classified briefing where we were notified that night goggles used in Vietnam were damaging to the eyes, which might not show up for many years. I asked how we were going to identify and notify those soldiers who had been exposed to this potential danger. My words made the others in the room very uncomfortable. And then I was notified that this was classified information that could not be shared. This was my introduction to the cover-up regarding known dangers being kept secret from the American people, in this case American soldiers. It was also my first introduction to light energy that can cause blindness.

Back in 1976, I was introduced to an insider's insider who decided I had to know something beyond Top Secret. It was planned that an intricate communications system would be introduced as advanced technology enhancing what we now call telecommunications. But the real purpose was to use electromagnetic energy to control the population. This honestly terrified me. We would be placed in an electronic prison. At the time they called it a "psyonics weapon". Today we call it 5G.

Even after getting out of the active Army, I continued to watch the buildup of the telecommunications industry. I was also reading the research coming out regarding the dangers associated with these new systems. Back in the 1980s, the concern amongst those calling for caution and more research was primarily regarding the electric system. A major concern was the huge towers and wires running close to schools and residential areas. But even the refrigerator with its low-level electromagnetic radiation was found to be dangerous, especially to children.

And then I discovered that technicians and operators of military radars were coming down with way too many, very rare, brain cancers. This was just an added note on the growing dangers being documented. When I was 33, my brother Phil finally opened up somewhat about his job as a Navy civilian. It turns out he was working on radars. I felt like I got hit in the head. I tried to explain the dangers to him and he gave me that "yeah right" look and dismissed me. It took 23 years before he died of a brain tumor that was fairly rare at that time. The same tumor is now directly linked to microwave emissions and is way too prevalent. I suddenly had blood in the game. Nobody wanted to listen. It was an inconvenient truth.

With nobody listening and no obvious solution other than dismantling the technology, I stopped worrying and got on with life for the next 35 years. And then I was introduced to Shungite and Walt Silva who explained the reason the signals were toxic was the direction they wrapped the copper wire at the very beginning of the system. I soon realized Shungite was going to level the playing field. Shungite could change the toxic and damaging spin of electric and electronic signals to make them biocompatible with life. We could stop the onslaught of electronic fog without dismantling the technology. The game was on again!

GAIA'S GIFT

So what was I doing for 35 years not actively fighting EM pollution? For the first 25 years, I was a maintenance engineer for a 500 unit condominium directly on the beach in Hallandale, Florida. Working hours of midnight to 8 A.M. allowed me time to research Metaphysics. It was a cool job. Seldom did I have to do anything more than check on the Boiler Room equipment. Seldom was it required for me to answer an emergency. But every day I saw the sun rise over the Atlantic Ocean. And every night I was reading books on metaphysical and esoteric thought and a few other subjects.

The Universe of Spiritual Intervention works in mysterious ways. Who would have imagined that a gift of an amethyst pendant in May 1988 would result in my opening the Shungite Internet Store called "Gaia's Gift" 34 years later?

I had been wearing the amethyst pendant for a few days and started detecting subtle changes in my body. I do not remember where the book came from, but it was a small book on minerals and strangely had an introduction to the way their energies can affect us! The physical symptoms that could be experienced were listed and all of my detected changes were on the list. This book and the pendant sent me into the Mineral Kingdom.

My next-door neighbor and best friend Sandi was the one who gave me the amethyst pendant. I told her what had happened and gave her the book. By 1992 I was engaged in buying and selling minerals and gemstones. This was also the time I learned how to wrap nuggets with wire to make pendants. The problem was, I could buy but I could not sell. Even if I decided to sell something, if I did not like the customer I would not sell it. So my excursion into the retail business did not last long, but I had developed very good connections to the suppliers of very special minerals.

I ended up with a rather large collection of some of the most stunning minerals and gemstones available. And more than I like to think about, I bought and then was led to put them in the yard and I have not seen them since.

The fact that I could not sell was because I did not see minerals in any form as inanimate things. Along my journeys I had come to accept that consciousness and life are much more complex than most people understand. Minerals, as well as plants, have energy signatures. It is these signatures that are blueprints for whatever form is manifesting. Human beings and animals, minerals, and all forms of the plant kingdom have energy fields. And while each energy field is different, these energy fields are all built from the same basic reservoir of energy. A Ruby has the signature of Ruby. And very often we need the same energy contained in Ruby.

Years before, I had already played with pyramid power. As I delved deeper and deeper into the mineral world and the esoteric writings concerning their energies that have the power to be beneficial to health, it became obvious minerals and pyramids should be brought together. I started building energy devices and spent many years doing so.

To give you an understanding of how far this went, one of the devices resulted in South Florida being hit with thousands of bolts of lightning within an hour. This caused the television stations to broadcast warnings. A friend of mine, who knew what I was working on, saw the broadcast and put it together in his head that I may be the one causing it. He called, I ran and stopped the device. There were no more warnings and no explanation by the press for this unprecedented strange phenomenon.

I had also begun working with minerals to make elixirs. In the same way that homeopathy uses the plant kingdom to isolate their energy signature, minerals can be soaked in water with the same results. It turns out that water has the ability to store energy. This is why homeopathy works. With my collection of minerals I was able to create more than three dozen mineral elixirs. They range from the basic ones of Ruby, Emerald, and Amethyst down to minerals not normally seen.

It is important to understand that during the same time frame I was being introduced to the concept that we all have spiritual guides and it is a Universe of Spiritual Intervention. I can point to so many things that were absolutely contrived to give me information or direction. I am a very rational, reasonable person and also very detailed oriented. But I get something in my head and it just will not go away unless I actually build or consider something.

So one night I come home from work and I start getting what I call "downloads". I just did what I was instructed to do. I got an unopened gallon of water in a plastic container and began putting a dozen different mineral energies in it in the form of elixirs, and sometimes the rock itself. As a final touch, they had me stick an energy device that was a two-foot long rod into the water container. As instructed, I left the gallon of water outside overnight.

The next morning I completely forgot about it. And then the voice started, "Go get it." I actually asked, "Go get what?" And then I remembered and went out and was stunned when I felt absolutely nothing special about the water, even with the energy device still in it. This was confounding as I figured it should be extremely energetic. Even after drinking a bit of it I did not feel any energy signature.

Shortly after that my house-mate woke up and I greeted him with a glass of water. He graciously tried the water. I saw a change in the container of water as he was sipping the water while listening to me explain what it was. It appeared that human interaction with the energized water was required to activate it.

The next day, two friends attended a big health fair kind of event. I sent them with a spray bottle of this energized water. All during the day they would spritz people who agreed to it. Back here, I watched that gallon of water become more and more energized as the day went on.

I named it "Nectar" and transferred the water from the plastic container into a glass jug. With the exception of a few ounces, that gallon of water is sitting in front of me, well actually above me, on the shelf. That was 25 years ago and the water still looks pristine. I have to admit that I have not tested it, but I am pretty sure it is still pure water holding some amazing energies.

Just before this, I had met a man named Barry who was also into mineral energies. He and I began to test this new form of energy. We had a medical doctor with PhDs in three medical specialties who happened to be interested in alternative healing modalities. We had discovered a way of transferring the energies of the Nectar into foam used to make innersoles you put in shoes. A local company manufactured shoe innersoles, and we had a short run made where Nectar water was added during production.

The foam innersoles held the energy charge. The doctor arranged for half a dozen of his clients to come by his office right after work. He took stress tests and all of them were extremely stressed from a day at work. We had them put innersoles in their own shoes while they were still on the stress machine. Within two minutes the stress meter started going down. Within five minutes no stress was detected in any of the six patients.

These results got us into the Florida International University sports center. Athletes were tested without and then with the innersoles in their shoes. The results concluded that the athletes did much better with the innersoles. So my would-be partner used those results to convince the Nike Footwear manufacturing company to test the innersole at their facilities. After a year, Nike said no thanks. I found out about this only after my partner had divorced his wife, who remained my friend.

It appears Nike could not understand why these innersoles were so effective and had no comprehension of how they could advertise them. Instead of coming to me, my partner managed to blow an awesome opportunity to make an extreme difference in the way we look at health. He did not understand and could not explain the concept of energy healing and enhancement.

Bummer, but it is all in the timing. Sometimes you get really close to something and fail because a more perfect situation is coming. And to get to that better place you need to fail and gain the necessary knowledge for the project you are really here to manifest. If it was not for Nectar I would not have so easily understood Shungite.

The concept that we could charge foam, which is 30% water, led us to try energy transference to other substances. The first powder we tried was calcium chloride, a chemical compound used in pool water to balance pH. It was safe and held the energies the same way the foam had.

One of the most impressive things that Nectar taught me was how very little of it could make a difference in a very large swimming pool. A friend had a pool in their condominium complex and we were over there one Saturday with all these loud and kind of obnoxious children in the pool. On a whim, I added a touch of the Nectar powder and suddenly every child was full of joy and the noise became laughter.

I had put the powder in the palm of my hand and then put my hand in the water and sloshed it around. As I did this, I was immediately aware that the water had become softer, or at least that's how I interpreted the change. Now I would explain it as the entire pool having become charged with an amazing energy called Nectar.

After that I was like Johnny Appleseed, only I was putting nectar in every swimming pool I could find. Instead of planting apple trees I was planting energy. One night I went to the condominium and found the pool being refilled and I had to tend to it. This was a huge pool, one of the biggest I have ever seen, and it took all night to fill. In the morning I asked the pool manager why he had emptied the pool. He said somebody had an accident, i.e. they had crapped in the pool. By law that required the pool to be completely drained. I offhandedly remarked, "I guess I'd better put some of my magic powder in it again."

He looked like I had hit him in the back of the head. "That's what's happening!" he exclaimed. He then explained how they could not understand why so many people had been coming down to the pool every day and not getting out all day long.

At this time I did not pursue Nectar in the way it deserved. All these metaphysical and energy and mineral things were more of a hobby and life got in the away. But I learned about the magic of mineral energies. When Shungite came into my life, I was not particularly surprised. It took very little time to feel and to learn that Shungite was something special. I recognized it. I think USI sent the Nectar to train me in readiness for a rock that contained the same energy and much more.

I was ready for Shungite. Lee Brown brought it to me. Within a month the internet Shungite Store called "Gaia's Gift" went live on May 4th, 2014. By Fall 2014, Walt and I were working together and five years later we have a book called *Shungite Reality*.

14. Shungite Energy Devices can be created for very specific purposes.

Walt Silva had also been investigating energy. While I was concentrating on pyramids and minerals and then Nectar, Walt was focusing on Orgone Energy Devices. A note here, "Orgone" was coined by Dr. Wilhelm Reich. "Orgonite" is actually a trademarked name for products that are essentially orgone devices.

The many hundreds of wrapped pendants I made using a variety of different minerals and gemstones were made by wrapping the nugget or gem in a way that best worked with the shape of whatever I was wrapping. The Shungite was different. There was an energy signature present in every single nugget and it was very specific in the direction it moved. Sometimes the nugget looks better as an ornamental piece the opposite way that I wrap it.

Initially, I was not aware that the wire also had an energy running through it and in a very specific direction. It was by focusing on the movement of energy in the Shungite nuggets that made me see energy that was moving in the same direction in the wire. The energy flow in both the nugget and the wire needs to be in the same direction to get the optimal positive energy circulation. Walt was able to identify that the energy flowing through the wire is orgone and it is attracted at one end of a wire and sent out the other end.

By the time I met Walt in September 2014, he had created a variety of energy devices based on orgone. His website NewParadigmTools.net begins this way:

> As the Earth shifts into a new state, with new ways of thinking and feeling, this has brought forth tools for the paradigm of the New Energy, where we can address the state of the "intangible" vibrations that surround us every day.
>
> The new tools are the product of combining the energy attributes and properties of geometric bodies (such as pyramids and cones) with materials that work to attract, transmute and counteract "stagnant" and "depleting" energy from a living or work space.
>
> These can be and have been used for energy work and other kinds of healing work.

Walt had sent me a couple of his devices and they were extremely powerful energetic turbines, for lack of another word. And then he sent me what he called the "Shungite Spirit Spiral". This was the first of many Shungite-Orgone devices designed to radiate specific energies.

These spirals are all made in the same way. Walt takes copper tubing 1/4 inch in diameter and rotates it to make a spiral. Orgone energy is attracted at one end of the tubing and begins to move through the tubing. Between the beginning and the end of the spiral, Walt put together Shungite, and later Shungite and magnets, between the two ends. This now closed circuit has integrated orgone, magnets and Shungite energy.

If you look at the strings on a guitar, they are all the same length but the thickness changes. The changes in thickness create the differences in the notes produced by the strings. In the piano, there are different strings with different thicknesses, but they also have different lengths. Whether it is length or thickness, what is being changed is the frequency of the sound being transmitted by the vibrating string.

In Walt's spiral devices, it is the length of the copper tubing that changes. He is able to determine what length of copper tubing equates to the frequency of energy to be emitted by the device. Walt determined that a specific length of copper tubing equated to the frequency of Shungite. He made the Shungite Spirit Spiral to emit that frequency. He also went on to make devices that would radiate anything from a pink rose to love. Throughout 2015, Walt produced dozens of one-of-a-kind spirals, which he sent to me. Even though they were all constructed exactly the same, except for the length of the tubing, none of them had the same energies.

Walt has gone on to make some stunning devices. We sell two of them in the Cosmic Reality Shungite Store, called "Gaia's Gift" - the Shungite Water Turtle and The Shungite Turpentine Spiral. You can contact Walt to purchase other Shungite energy devices at newparadigmtools.net. Our mission has remained to get Shungite to the masses but Walt could not possibly get an orgone device to every human on the planet. Walt also has a weekly internet radio show called "Cosmic Reality Radio Show". Radio show archives and current shows can be found at CosmicReality.com.

15. Does Shungite have sentience?

We were on live radio and nearing the end of the second hour. Walt said to me, "I have something I'm going to put in the mail to you tomorrow."

"What is it?" I asked.

"I really don't know. It got into my head and I had to build it and you're the one that needs to figure out what it is and how it works. But I have to get it out of here. It gave me a very bad burn."

"What do you mean it gave you a burn? Well wait, we will talk after the show."

So instead of hanging up on Skype after the show, Walt turned on the video and held up a six-inch by six-inch cube of resin containing six implosion coils. Even over video or looking at a picture on the Internet, a photograph, or in this case a cube, the energy field can be felt. Whatever this cube was it was powerful, and even if I could not feel the energy, one look at Walt Silva's face was enough to convince me this was one powerful device. He looked like he had a 2nd degree burn on his face.

Walt was holding up this cube in front of the camera, and behind the camera his face was as red as I could imagine it being without having physical damage. I silently asked

"Gaia, what do I tell him?' I hear a voice that says, "tell him to turn it off."

I repeated, "Turn it off."

"How do I do that?"

"Just tell it to turn off!"

Walt bowed his head and concentrated while I did the same, trying to make the cube shut down. After a minute, he opened his eyes, looked up and said, "It's still on." This surprised me as I detected it was in the off position.

"I think it has a residual field. Put it on the floor to ground it." Walt bent down and I could not see him anymore. A minute or so later, he sat upright with the cube still in his hands. His face had no indication of redness.

This was the beginning of our understanding of what Walt coined the "sentience" of Shungite. The Webster definition that seems to match our observations of Shungite is:

> Definition of sentient
>
> 1: responsive to or conscious of sense impressions

But this is a very vague definition. So let's look at definition 2 that equates sentient to the word "aware", and aware is defined as:

> 2: having or showing realization, perception, or knowledge

This is what we have observed:

1. Shungite reacts to thought.

2. It knows the difference between beneficial thought and negative thought.

3. Shungite enhances positive thoughts by providing direct access to quantum proto-energy.

4. Shungite will simply turn off if it does not resonate with the person trying to use it.

We initially focused on these qualities while interacting with the Shungite-Orgone Devices Walt was making. It was obvious the devices could essentially interact with certain people. It appeared the only limitation of where that interaction could go was the imagination of the person working with it.

It was our customers' observations and experiences even more than our own, that made Walt declare there is a sentience in Shungite. I do not know if it is sentience, but I do know that many people make an emotional connection to Shungite energy devices and even the nuggets themselves.

A friend who had Shungite from me watched her husband take his keys out of his pocket and accidentally the Shungite nugget fell to the ground and bounced under the car. The husband got on his hands and knees and began virtually crawling under the car. She yelled to him that they had more Shungite. He yelled back, "But this is MY Shungite."

This takes the concept of "Pet Rock" to a new level, and you know what, I totally get it. I have rocks, pendants, spirals, and cubes that I have been blessed to meet and work with. They are family and friends and colleagues working for the same purpose I am - to get Shungite to the masses. Shungite is a profound gift. We have been able to make energy devices built upon a cosmic construction that came to Earth and sat for 2.5 billion years until humanity had evolved to the degree that we could believe in magic. And magic is just the manipulation of energy.

You do not have to believe that Shungite has a sentience, for lack of a better word, to have it purify your water and make EM/WiFi/radioactive frequencies biocompatible. This is just energy in action.

But we need much more to stop the Sixth Extinction Event.

The 5G Death March

The race to get the 5G Network deployed changed the game once again. As early as 2014, I was warning of its dangers. However, I was also in a race to get Shungite to the masses and not focused on what I soon termed the 5G Death March. By 2019, I had no option but to turn my attention to what would finalize the Sixth Extinction Event. I knew Shungite could NOT mitigate 5G signals. The Sixth Extinction Event was being driven by the existing 4G system. The only hope I had was that the Shungite Bees might be able to wake people up before it was too late to stop 5G and turn around the ongoing devastation from 4G.

As telecommunication systems have spread, so has the death of the insects spread. It is difficult to monitor the microorganisms and insects, except in the case of the Honeybees where the bees are kept and counted. The Shungite Beehives Project demonstrated Shungite can reverse the die-off and accelerate the expansion of the Honeybee community. The only explanation for this expansion is that the telecommunication signals were attenuated to become biocompatible and less toxic to the Honeybees. If the bees can be saved by Shungite, perhaps the Sixth Extinction Event that is ongoing can be reversed.

- Nancy Hopkins

CHAPTER 5
Shungite, the Bees and the Sixth Extinction Event

By the time we got to 2017, I was on radio asking for beekeepers to contact me. I was convinced that the decline in the worldwide bee population was directly due to the proliferation of telecommunications systems. There was a correlation between the decline of the Honeybees and the spread of WiFi communications.

The bee presented the perfect opportunity to test out Shungite's ability to attenuate EM/WiFi signals. They, and all insects, are much more vulnerable to physical damage due to WiFi signals, and the ability for bees to navigate using the natural energy terrain was more and more difficult because of the proliferation of electronic signals saturating the environment.

Colony Collapse Disorder had appeared. Healthy hives would suddenly be abandoned. The worker bees simply failed to return to the hive to care for the queen and the brood of eggs and young bees. This was a worldwide phenomenon and could not be directly linked to increases in poisons from fertilizers and pesticides. Nor was it a sudden loss of habitat. The one thing found all over the world where bees were disappearing was the spread of 4G WiFi.

Derek Condit, The Bee Guy

Derek Condit heard me calling out to beekeepers and he answered the call. He was new to beekeeping as he had his first two hives in 2016 which he raised without any chemicals. As happens to many if not most beekeepers, he lost the bees over the winter. By spring 2017, Derek's two brand new hives had three Shungite nuggets at the entrance to the hive. This was the first Shungite Apiary and it is located in Washington State, USA.

The Universe of Spiritual Intervention was in action and Derek and I became connected. By September 2018, we reestablished the Cosmic Reality company in Washington where Derek and his wife Maureen took over running the internet store and product production.

The Sixth Extinction

Do you know that humanity and the planet are experiencing the "Sixth Extinction Event"? Scientists have identified five previous mass extinctions with 75-96% loss of life starting 375 million years ago. So it is likely that Earth will keep going, but a large portion of humanity and many species of animals and plants and microorganisms will simply disappear. The areas that survive will be those where man's technological death is not present.

This extinction event is all manmade. It is directly attributable to the proliferation of WiFi systems. Animals, plants, and microorganisms are vanishing at an astounding rate. The loss of large animal species is well known - but this is associated with loss of habitat and other factors. What was being missed was the total destruction of insects and microorganisms.

The Honeybee is on the verge of extinction and in many regions there is a 90% loss. The Royal Geographical Society of London concluded that bees are the most important living being on the planet. 70% of plants need the bee's pollination to survive. Animals need the plants to survive. Where goes the bee go we all. The Federal Institute of Technology of Switzerland has pointed to WiFi frequencies as the problem. They are only one organization among many making this connection.

Why Is EMF/WiFi Radiation Damaging?

Everything on Earth has a specific vibration or frequency. All humans, animals, plants, and insects have a certain vibrational field that has to be maintained at a specific level to remain healthy.

NASA and other space agencies have been using frequency generators for decades to protect astronauts while they are away from the Earth's natural frequency source. Astronauts' physical and mental health deteriorated while in outer space, away from the Schumann Resonance (Earth's frequency). This problem was solved by introducing the "Schumann Simulator", a magnetic pulse generator broadcasting the Earth's natural frequency, into all space shuttles.

Unfortunately, today's technologies, such as computer monitors, laptops, tv's, radios, microwave ovens, Wi-Fi routers, smart meters, and cell-phones all use electromagnetic waves in order to function. We live in an environment polluted with electromagnetic energy. This unnatural energy does have negative effects on the minds and neurological systems of humans and animals. There is irrefutable scientific proof that many mental and physical ailments are directly linked to EM/WiFi/RF radiation.

These frequencies are also extremely harmful to the bees. When the bees' vibration field or frequency is disharmonious, their meridian clocks are disturbed, immunity is compromised, natural recovery and rejuvenation abilities are reduced, and their overall wellness suffers. This was seen when there were only 3G WiFi systems. This breakdown in the bees makes them more susceptible to diseases, pests and chemical toxins. But in areas with high-power WiFi radiation, the Colony Collapse Disorder began proliferating. Hives were deserted for no apparent reason.

The following comes from one test that was conducted: "Exposure to Cell Phone Radiations Produces Biochemical Changes in Worker Honey Bees" by Neelima R. Kumar, Sonika Sangwan, and Pooja Badotra. This report was looking specifically at "...the metabolic changes with respect to proteins, carbohydrates, and lipids in the hemolymph of worker honeybee."

The real goal was to determine the extent of health damages due to cell phones. The researchers chose the Honeybee because "Honeybees are reliable indicators of environmental status and... are the best experimental animals to study the effect of electromagnetic waves." They subjected the bees to 40 minutes of two identical phones connected to the same network while one was playing a recording and the other was listening.

While absolutely seeing changes in what they were looking at, maybe the best observation is this:

> *It was interesting to note that during the present study, as the exposure time increased, it appeared that the bees having assessed the source of the disturbance decided to move and a large scale movement of the workers toward the talk-mode (not toward the listening mobile) was observed. Also, the bees became slightly aggressive and started beating their*

wings in agitation. - "Exposure to Cell Phone Radiations Produces Biochemical Changes in Worker Honey Bees" by Neelima R. Kumar, Sonika Sangwan, and Pooja Badotra

Swiss researcher Daniel Favre made the connection between WiFi and bee decline back in 2009. In his study, Favre placed cell phones in Honeybee hives and observed what happened when the phones were active, inactive, powered down, or ringing. As soon as the phone was ringing or active the bees reacted in confusion and moved to leave the hive that contained the phone. For 12 hours after the phone was off, the bees were demonstrating the same confusion and desire to escape. Another experiment showed the dramatic consequences of a phone in a hive.

> *"In one experiment, it was found that when a mobile phone was kept near a beehive it resulted in a collapse of the colony in 5 to 10 days,"* says Favre, *"with the worker bees failing to return home, leaving the hives with just queens, eggs, and hive-bound immature bees."* (- this is called "Colony Collapse Disorder or CCD.)

Favre and his team at the Swiss Federal Institute of Technology conducted 83 separate tests to observe the bees' reaction to cellphone signals. The reaction was due to an increase in worker bees' piping noise that normally signals the bees to leave the hive. But instead of a swarm of bees manifesting due to the hive becoming over-populated, the test bees appeared confused and disoriented. Favre's study confirmed an earlier 2008 study concluding the bees would not return to a hive if the cellphone was nearby and operating.

The obvious conclusion is that bees react to EMF/WiFi signals. If the signals are targeting the hive, the bees leave. The fact that there is a correlation between the proliferation of cellular technology and the Colony Collapse Disorder (CCD) is not surprising. In a CCD situation, the worker bees do not return to the hive and the queen, a few nurse bees, immature bees, larvae, and food are just abandoned.

Technology authorities will tell you that this CCD and loss of bees is not due to WiFi. And cases are made all the time that it is chemical toxins and climate change that are the cause. Dr. Sainudeen Sahib.S Associate Professor, PG & Research Dept. Of Zoology, S.N.College, Kollam, Kerala in India presented a report in 2010 entitled "Electromagnetic Radiation (EMR) Clashes with Honey Bees". He is considered an Indian Government expert on the possible impact of mobile towers on living beings. Dr. Sainudeen Sahib.S, turned to the honey bee, as we have, to test his fears about WiFi radiation.

Dr. Sainudeen Sahib.S points to the fact that bees have been in existence for at least 100 million years. Science confirms there have been similar planet-wide climate changes due to heating caused by a build-up of CO_2, and past examples of rapid increase in carbon emissions (just like today) were generally highly destructive to life on Earth. As is happening now, those abrupt temperature changes resulted in mass extinctions. But the bees have survived. Today they are on the brink of extinction. So climate change does not seem to be the source of the bee extinction threat. And the other proclaimed culprit - chemical assault - also does not work. The die-off is too widespread and too connected to areas with WiFi proliferation to be chemically induced.

Bees and other insects have survived and evolved complex immune system on this planet over a span of millions of years. It is not logical that they would now suddenly die out now due to diseases and natural parasites. This suggests another factor has been introduced to their environment that disrupts their immune system. This man made factor is the mobile towers and mobile phones.

New experiments suggests a strong correlation between population decline and cellular equipment. . The massive amount of radiation produced by towers and mobile phones is actually frying the navigational skills of the honey bees and preventing them from returning back to their hives. The thriving hives suddenly left with only queens, eggs and hive bound immature worker bees. Thus electromagnetic radiation exposure provides a better explanation for Colony Collapse Disorder (CCD) than other theories. The path of CCD in India has followed the rapid development of cell phone towers, which cause atmospheric electromagnetic radiation.

Insects and other small animals would naturally be the first to obviously be affected by this increase in ambient radiation since naturally they have smaller bodies and hence less flesh to be penetrated by exposure to microwaves. The behavioral pattern of bees alters when they are in close proximity to mobile phones and towers. The vanished bees are never found, but thought to die singly far from home. Bee keepers told that several hives have been abruptly abandoned. If towers and mobile phones increase the honey bees might be wiped out in ten years. Radiation of 900 MHZ is highly bioactive, causing significant alternation in the physiological function of living organisms

- Dr. Sainudeen Sahib.S: INTERNATIONAL JOURNAL OF ENVIRONMENTAL SCIENCES Volume 1, No 5, 2011

The study used 3 control hives without mobile phones while 3 test hives were subjected to WiFi radiation. For ten days, for ten minutes per day, the 3 test hives were radiated with 900 MHZ from a standard cell phone. The response was determined by counting eggs and monitoring how many worker bees left and returned to the hive every minute. These figures were compared to data before and after exposure to WiFi. The results are summarized as follows.

3. Results

The results of the studies are presented in the Table below. The present study showed that **after ten days the worker bees never returned to hives in the test colonies**. *It was shown that the total bee strength was significantly higher in the control colonies, being nine comb frames, compared to only one in the test colony at the end of the experiment.* **The thriving hives were suddenly left with only queens, eggs, and hive-bound immature worker bees. The queens in the test colonies produced fewer eggs/day (100) compared to the control hive (350).** *It has previously been reported that there is a low egg laying rate in queens exposed to high voltage transmission lines and* exposure of the queen bees to cell phone radiation stimulated them to produce only drones. **Thus, electromagnetic radiation (EMR) exposure provides a better explanation for Colony Collapse Disorder (CCD) than other theories.**

Table 1: Change in colony status of honeybees exposed to mobile phones

Parameter	Control (mean ± SD)	Treated (10 m exposure for 10 days.
(No. of worker bees leaving the hive entrance/ minute)		
Before exposure	40.7±15	38.2±12
During exposure	41.5±14	18.5±13
After exposure	42.4±14	Nil
Returning ability		
Before exposure	42.5±15	39.5±14
During exposure	43.6±14	15.6±13
After exposure	44.6±13	Nil
Bee strength		
Before exposure	9 Frame	9 Frame
During exposure	9 Frame	5 Frame
After exposure	9 Frame	I Frame
Egg laying rate of queen /day		
Before exposure	365.25	355.10
During exposure	362.15	198.60
After exposure	350.15	100.00

- Dr. Sainudeen Sahib.S: INTERNATIONAL JOURNAL OF ENVIRONMENTAL SCIENCES Volume 1, No 5, 2011

To make the point, there was no CCD prior to activation of the WiFi for 10 minutes over 10 days. After exposure to the WiFi radiation, the hives were abandoned. So much for chemical poisoning as the source of CCD. It is WiFi and the entire spectrum of telecommunications systems that are the direct cause of the near extinction of the Honeybees. Think logically! There was no CCD before WiFi, either in this experiment or in the rest of the world.

But, unlike the drastic loss of life in a WiFi environment, for the bees in a Shungite Environment there is only hive expansion, with no loss of life due to CCD, disease of any kind or losses attributed to parasites.

Shungite and the Honeybees

3.5 billion years ago life began on Earth. 2.5 billion years ago Earth was struck by a meteor that landed in what is now Western Russia in an area called Karelia. That deposit of a mineral mixture is called Shungite after the small town in the area called Shunga. It looks like a coal deposit, stretching 1,000 square kilometers and up to 400 feet deep. Shungite has been proven to detoxify water, soil, and air. It also negates radiation in the form of natural and nuclear radiation and electromagnetic radiation.

If bees do not want something on or near the hive, they simply move it out of the way. The Honeybees given Shungite nuggets by their caretaker Derek Condit liked their Shungite so much, they glued the three nuggets to the hive using propolis. And, going in or out of the hive, the bees would walk over to the Shungite nuggets and rub up against them. By the end of the 2017 season, the bees' continual rubbing had worn the nuggets down to shapes like little mountains.

So what happened? Beginning 5/20/17 in an 11 week time frame, the first 2 hives went from 50,000 bees to an estimated half-million bees in a total of **8 hives** and an unknown number of swarmed bees in the wild. There was also no disease, mites or Colony Collapse, even though neighboring apiaries reported both Nosema disease and Varroa mites.

Here is the summary of the sequence of events:

5/20/17: Three Shungite Nuggets were placed on the right side of the entrance to two beehives. The year before, bees from Derek's first hives had not survived the winter. Starting again with two new hives and new bees, Derek added three medium-sized Shungite nuggets to the right side of the hive entrance. At no time were any chemicals used.

6/1/17: Derek noticed that both hives were beginning to exhibit signs of swarming, despite there being an empty box with empty frames on top of the brood box (so there was room for expansion). After opening the top of the hive, Derek found both hives making queen bee cells. It was approximately three weeks after receiving the nuggets that hive #1 produced queens. It takes around three weeks for a queen to be produced, so it appears the queens were begun at approximately the same time that the nuggets were introduced.

Derek made preparations for the expansion of the hives by building four new hives. By moving frames filled with honey or eggs and bees into the new hives, the two starting hives were now six hives. Queens from the original two hives were born into a Shungite environment and are considered the first generation Shungite Bee. Their babies were the first generation conceived and born with Shungite.

Before building the four new hives, Derek decided to add Shungite Bee Powder to one of the hives. The powder was placed in two small plastic trays, with .75g in each, at the entrance of beehive #1 only. Approximately 2-3 hours later, 90% of the powder had been carried away by the bees, who had immediately begun walking through it.

6/24/17: Approximately three weeks after Shungite Bee Powder was introduced to hive #1, queens were again being produced. This time they swarmed before Derek could respond to the massive expansion in the hive. He had to capture the swarm or ball of bees and put it into another newly constructed hive. A second swarm was also captured and there were now eight hives.

In the next few weeks, the bee colonies continued expanding and swarming into the surrounding environment. In the wild, the Shungite Bees helped strengthen other bee communities. As the cooler Fall weather began settling in, the birth rate of the bees declined. By the time winter arrived, Derek had consolidated the smaller bee communities into 5 hives.

Derek estimated that the original hives of 50,000 bees had expanded to 500,000 bees recaptured into hives and an additional 500,000 in the wild. This was accomplished in 11 weeks with three Shungite nuggets on each hive and three applications of Shungite Bee Powder.

This first Shungite apiary was on rented property. In February 2018, Derek bought a uniquely perfect property with a house and three garage-size, metal buildings on it. It is located in the middle of the Cascade Mountains in Washington State, US. The new apiary was situated inside one of the buildings, with the openings of the hive up against slits in the metal walls. By Spring 2018, due to natural losses during the winter, Derek had just one Shungite hive from the 2017 season.

Derek ordered nucs of bees from California to start two additional hives in Spring 2018. These bees were sick and contaminated by chemical treatments. The small nucs, which are like small hives that are used to start full-sized hives, were stained with chemicals and diarrhea from the sick bees. The bees were also very aggressive.

The new hives were set up with Shungite nuggets next to the one remaining 2017 Shungite hive. Over a period of a couple of weeks, Derek replaced the dirty hive frames with new frames and the aggression of the new bees disappeared.

All was going extremely well. The new hives thrived along with the original Shungite community. But in 2018, Derek was being inundated with requests to talk about Shungite Beehives and essentially could not keep up with the swarming bees.

This 2018 Shungite Beehives season turned out to be an excellent demonstration of what happens when a million bees enter the surrounding environment. As the Condits were new to the town, neighbors made sure to point out that the vast amounts of foliage, fruit and flowers were not normal. In fact, the amount of produce and its quality was something "new". Old apple trees were so full of fruit that their limbs broke.

The best story was about the wild grapes. The roots are in the neighbor's yard but the grapevine is all over the fence and in Derek's yard. The neighbor warned Derek that the local moonshiner would be checking out the grapes. He never used them as they were small, dry and were not worthy enough to make good moonshine, but he did make a point of checking them out.

When the moonshiner did show up after sundown...well it was a bit tense at first until Derek realized who it was and then there was just friendship. The moonshiner was amazed at the grapes which were at least three times as big and sweet and tasty. Derek wished him well on his moonshine endeavors, grateful the grapes were gone, because the dogs liked to eat them and grapes are not good for dogs.

Derek's 2017 and 2018 experiences from simply adding Shungite nuggets to the hives resulted in no losses of any abnormal kind. There were no instances of CCD, mites or diseases, although neighboring apiaries had them. And during the winter between the two seasons, three of the five hives survived an abnormally cold winter with abnormal amounts of snow. No other beekeeper reported any of their hives surviving. In addition, the Shungite Bees had a population expansion that is way beyond normal.

What this demonstrated was confirmation of what had been known about Shungite for hundreds of years. Shungite transmutes toxins and provides an environment for enhanced health. Our research determined that this phenomenon was due to Shungite's powerful energy field that overpowered other forms of energy from toxic molecules, radioactive ions, and most electromagnetic signals. The result was a change in rotation of the toxic fields. Molecules could not make the adjustment and the molecules lost molecular cohesion, falling apart into harmless atoms. Due to the presence of Shungite, EM/WiFi signals simply reversed the rotation of their signal from harmful to biocompatible.

The Shungite Beehives

As an Internet Radio host and guest, the message about Shungite could be taken to thousands of listeners. While not always speaking about Shungite, it was certainly our favorite subject.

When Derek and the bees entered the story, we designated him "The Bee Guy" and put him on the radio to share his Shungite Bee stories. As I write this it is July 2019, and there are now Shungite Beehives worldwide. We only know about a sample of the many beekeepers who may be using Shungite with their bees. Derek is regularly invited to other countries to talk about the Shungite Bees. There may be failures somewhere, but we have only heard from one beekeeper who said their bees knocked the Shungite nuggets off the hive. Every other report confirms the same results that Derek got.

Although the 2018 Shungite hives survived a brutal winter, a false spring killed them. The weather got warm and the bees broke the bee ball that had kept the queen and a healthy number of worker bees alive during the cold. The workers went to work and then the cold returned. Without protection from the bee ball, they were suddenly all lost to the cold.

The point here is that it was Nature, not Man, that killed the bees. The Shungite Bees, could they talk, would testify that Shungite saved them from Colony Collapse Disorder where EM/WiFi radiation "fried" their navigation systems. It also protected them from the collapse of their immune systems, which fight all diseases, and subsequent weakening. Strong bees can take care of mites. By the Summer of 2019, Shungite Beehives were worldwide. We know of one University with an ongoing research project looking at Shungite and the bees.

Conclusion

Honeybees are kept and counted, providing proof that Shungite nuggets can help protect them from the toxic WiFi of the current 4G systems. If this is true, certainly other forms of life would also be protected in a Shungite Environment. How can we quickly help all forms of nature survive until humanity wakes up to the insanity of dirty technology?

There are other ways of providing us with the communications we are now accustomed to that can be applied to turn around the Sixth Extinction. Among alternative systems is fiber optic cable. We do not have to continue down this WiFi death march that will become a race if 5G is allowed to be introduced. And please note: we are NOT talking about using Shungite in a 5G environment. This is an entirely different situation. Shungite cannot protect you from 5G, and, even it could, what kind of a world would be left? The only solution to 5G is to stop it.

The Shungite World Grid

People worldwide are putting Shungite nuggets in tens of thousands of places. There is an internet world map depicting a sampling of those locations that has over 129,093 views. Many more are spreading Shungite and not reporting it. Is this a trend that will falter and fade away? Not likely, as it has been ongoing since 2014 and just keeps growing.

But is it enough to simply spread Shungite nuggets throughout the world to stop the Sixth Extinction? Well, maybe yes... if we take another look at the bees.

Every bee has one objective, and that is to work to make the hive thrive. Their entire world is the beehive. For mankind, the hive is planet Earth. Unlike the bee, humans claim no responsibility for maintaining anything more than their family. We will not survive apart. A Honeybee cannot survive alone. The hive cannot survive through the winter cold without coming together in a ball, where shared body heat keeps the hive going until the warmth of spring.

Humanity is on the brink of unprecedented cold. The biosphere of Earth is collapsing as WiFi destroys the microorganisms in the soil, along with the plants and all types of insects due to their physical structures being more prone to EMF damage. When the insects die a cascading collapse will follow as larger and larger animals starve to death. Think of the food chain disappearing from the bottom to the top, and at the top is the human species.

In July 2019, humanity commemorated 50 years since a man stepped on the moon The plaque that was left says:

> *"Here men from the planet Earth first set foot upon the Moon July 1969, A.D. We came in peace for all mankind."*

We should give this some thought.

There has never been one day of peace in those 50 years upon this fragile, blue marble, as Earth was called by those who saw her from so far away in a vast galaxy. They could see Earth as one entity, in all its glory. Buckminster Fuller called it "Spaceship Earth" and asked why we would destroy the spaceship. I ask, why are we destroying the hive?

We have forsaken our responsibilities to strive to make the hive thrive. Our survival depends upon us viewing Life in a different way. Instead of greed and lust for power dictating our reality we must turn to a reality where Nature is of paramount importance. The Hive must thrive if we are to grow into the peaceful people the 50-year-old moon plaque alludes to. We must move away from the concept of service to self to one of service to the Hive, service to Earth.

Democracy is where individual freedoms are upheld. Communism/Socialism emphasizes that the group is paramount. Fascism/Totalitarianism puts an elite above anyone who is not one of them. We need a new way of operating. We need something like "Naturalism", where what is good for Nature is good for the group and the individual, and where there is no elite focused on destruction and control.

And this new mindset is starting to spread. Perhaps the most powerful aspect of both the bees and Shungite is their ability to draw people together. People researching Shungite suddenly find themselves waking up to the Sixth Extinction. People desperate to find a way to stop the biosphere collapse end up looking at Shungite Beehives.

Some would say this sounds like striving for a "hive mind" where everyone is controlled by it. I counter that we already live in a hive-minded society that dictates what we should think and who is our enemy. "That guy over there is your enemy. Go kill him." And off the armies go. "Your god is better than their god, hate them." Well, that is just stupid. Who cares as long as both Gods are loving entities? "You are nothing if you are not rich, famous and/or in control of someone". How did that work out for you?

And then you have myself and all those others saying, "Ah, something is very wrong here and you might want to look around." "Well they are crazy and everything is just fine," you tell yourself. And that is when I hear "insanity vs humanity" cruising through my mind.

Some say we are experiencing the final battle between Good and Evil. Maybe. Or maybe we are just being forced to grow up and take responsibility. The insanity has gone on way too long. The sociopaths running the hive are leading us to destruction. It is time to take our power back - one Shungite nugget at a time.

For the last three years, Shungite Bees have told their story and shown that Shungite can protect them. People spreading Shungite throughout the world are on a mission to prove that Shungite can also reverse the currently unfolding Sixth Extinction Event. My team of Shungite researchers has developed Shungite-based energy devices, clearing toxins from huge bodies of water and taking radiation out of the air. Shungite has taught us to dream big, as our potential is infinite.

Again, I think of those astronauts hurtling between Earth and the Moon 50 years ago. The vehicles containing them were run by computers only as sophisticated as today's watches, if that. Theirs was an absolutely impossible mission and yet they accomplished it over and over again.

Our mission is to turn around the Sixth Extinction. I believe mankind can do this. But we must come together with one ultimate goal. Every form of life must be respected and protected. We must protect the planet and all that call her "home". Ever wonder why we have not gone back to the moon in 50 years? Perhaps there is no reason to return to a place where no life exists.

How Do We Turn Around the 5G Death March?

The only way to stop the 5G Death March is to stop 5G. Sane people all over the world have taken to the courts and the streets to stop the 5G insanity. Microwaves from the 4G systems are what propelled us into the Sixth Extinction. 5G uses millimeter and sub-gigahertz signals that the telecommunications companies stated have NOT been tested for possible health hazards.

In areas where 5G is deployed, bees have been found dead and dying on the streets. Flocks of birds have suddenly fallen dead and dying on the ground. Human health deterioration is being recorded in frightening numbers. Reproduction worldwide is down and in areas with 5G declining birth rates have intensified.

Please, do not just take my word for this, do the research. This book is not about 5G, as that is a book in itself. To understand why 5G is being deployed without any health assessment by breaking laws fundamental to the Constitution and the Republic requires you to reevaluate everything you have been taught. A good place to start is with my book *Cosmic Reality,* Book 2 - *Down the Rabbit Hole.* While you can buy this through Amazon, you can also get a free PDF of the book at www.CosmicReality.net.

I am bringing this book to a close because there is an impressive demand for it.

I hope the first three chapters give you a ready reference and overview of Shungite - what it is, how it works, and what it will do for you.

The fourth chapter is a deeper look at Enerology and Shungite Science. We looked at sympathetic resonance and quantum entanglement as science and metaphysical thought.

In the fifth chapter, the concept of the Sixth Extinction Event is presented the way the bees see it, so to speak. The bees are dying in one reality and thriving in another. The decision as to which reality survives is up to each and every one of us. Do you want to wait and see what happens? Or do you want to pursue the truth to create an alternative reality?

Why not just take a chance that Shungite levels the playing field by its ability to expand and accelerate thought. Add some Shungite to the world grid. Buy Shungite products that can help mitigate the 4G saturation and get you mentally, physically and emotionally healthy enough to fight back. The fight is one for the planet and all she is.

INDEX

3-6-9 principle. 207

4G 136, 141, 225, 227, 245, 246

5G. 138, **141**, 211, 225, 242, **245**

acupuncture. 93, **168**

addicted to social media.. 84

air. 4, 236

algae. 146

aloe vera 128

American Medical Association **169**, 173

antibodies.. 166

antioxidants. 66, 183

anxiety. 64

anxious.. 65

asthma in children. 14

astral body. 165

astral travel.. . . . . 95, 121

attenuate definition.. 160

auto magnet 97

backache. 93

bacteria. 13, 103, 116, 131, **132**, 166

bad odors.. 131

beads.. . . . . **11,** 97, 118, **119, 151,** 199 bees. 227

Big Pharma. 169

bioelectromagnetic **28**, **38, 40,** 41-43, 159, 171, 204, 209

bioelectromagnetic bodies 158

birds. 72, 92, 245

bites, insect bites. 88

Bluetooth. 137

bracelet. 149, **151**

Buckminster Fuller. 9, 66, **196**, 243

Bucky Ball. 9

bush. 108-109

buzzing in ears, dog ears standing.. . . . . 59, 82

C60 Molecules. **8-10,** 20, 114, 121, 142-143,

148, 194-198, 201-203

cancer. 18-19, 89, 167, **171-175,** 205, **210-211**

Cater, Joseph H. 179

cat's water 48

chelation therapy 76

chicken.. 105

chlorine. 13, 22, 91, 111, 114, 130

clarity. 49, 60, 61

coherent. 21-22, 122, 131, 149, 151, **157-158**, 207

colonoscopy. 77

commercial use of Shungite............................. 13, 117

composite mineral 115

congestion... 54

cooking water.. 54

COPD... 49

Cosmic Reality 57, 61, 67, 69, 73, 77, 91, 94, 96,
97, 99, 103, **123**, 142, 203, 221, 222, 228, 246

Cosmic Silver pendant................................ 128-130

coughing stopped.. 51

Crohns Disease.. 49

dehydrated... 82, 101

dental plaque... 132

depression... 56, 166

Derek Condit............................ 42, 108, 158, **227**, 236

detox... 60

diabetes.. 90

directed energy weapons 177

dizziness... 59, 210

doggie dementia.. 103

dog's water bowl.. 46

Dolly Howard... 129

Dr. Richard Gerber................................. 164, 170

Dr. Semeon J. Tsirpursky............................. 9, 197

Dr. Raymond Royal Rife.................... 172-175, 179, 184, 210

Dr. Wang Su... 9

Dr. Wilhelm Reich................ 149, **174-175**, 177-179, 184, 2019

dream.. 90, 99

drinking water...................... 57, 81, 100, 116, **123**, 125, 126

ear infection... 82

efficiency............................. 37, 39, 71, 140, 154, 156

electric bills...................................... 37, 120, 179

electric outlet covers.............................. 39, 140, 206

Elite..................... **10,** 57, 109, 114-115, 126, 133, 147, 243

emotions....................................... 65, 165, 203

empath... 65

energy bill... 62

energy follows geometry........................... 20, 36, 204

energy healing............................. 145, 159, **167**, 174

Energy Healing Devices................................. 170

energy sensitive...................... 29, 73, 92, 131, 142, 149

energy usage.. 101

Enerology............................ **5,** 20, **101,** 119, 120,

145, **161, 163, 168,** 177, **180**, 182, 191, 200

environmental protection............................. 15, 39

ethereal fluidium...................................... 166

etheric, etheric body........................ 165, 166, 174, 209 eyes, eyes burning, eyes watering 48, 66, 78, 170, 211

fiber-optic. 138

fibromyalgia. 49

fish. 83

flashlight test. 11, 119

fog, brain fog. 49, 160, 212

Fountain of Youth. 14

free radicals. 131

Frequently Asked Questions **113**

frozen energy. 5, 170, 180

fruits. 72, 93

Fuller, Buckminster 9, 66, **196**, 243

Fukushima. 13

fullerene. 8-10, 194-197, 201

Gaia. 17, 59, 79, 94, 223

garden. 130, 152

gas 37, 39, 67, 80, 110, 111, 154, 156

genuine. 7, 119

Gerber, Dr. Richard 164, 170

glass. 26, 91, 101, 126, 131

glyphosate. 143-145

greasy film on pet bowls. 132

hair... 89, 101, 107, 125

headaches..................................... 47, 48, 52, 210

health benefits............................ 13, 14, 118, **160**, 208

herbal.. 168

homeopathy......................... 168-169, 170, 172, 214-215

hot flashes 69

hot spots 100

How do I care for my Shungite Pendant........................ 151

hummingbird.. 110

impurities removed from water, gas, fuel............... 130, 154, 156

Interstellar...................................... 8, 115, 201, 202

Invention Secrecy Act... 179

iron.................................... 13, 114, 115, 116, 130, 133

Jan Shaw 45

Karelia...................................... 2, 113, 198, 201, 208

kidney... 104, 106

Kirlian photographs 121, 123, 157, 207

knee ache.. 51, 90, 93

Kozyrev, Nikolai 153

Lake Onega 117

lawnmower... 68

Lee Brown.................................... 3, 17, 208, 219

Magic Frequency... 171

253

magnetic therapy 34

Maksovskaya deposit. 12

manganese. 130

Marcial Waters. 14

Mark Steele. 136

mass spectrometer. 197

Max Planck. 5, 181

metals. 13, 74, 76, 109, 116, 133

Metaphysics. 4, 119, 120

microorganisms. 116, 131, 132, 172

mildew. 53

Mind-Body Connection. 169

mold. 16, 45, 133, 143, **146**

molecular spin 124

mood. 63, 108

Mother Lode 116, 142, 148, 198, 199

muscle strain. 93

muscle testing. 144-145

negativity. 58, 70, 75

Nikola Tesla 157, 175-176, 180, 206

Nikolai Kozyrev 153

Nitrates and nitrites. 130

NO change in my meter 137

Noble. 10, 114, 147

nuggets. 150, 152, 156,-158, 160,

185, 187, 192, 198, 207, 213, 228, 236, 242

old dogs. 105

orgone. 40, 140, 149, 151, 153,

154, **174, 184-187**, 203-205, 219-222

Orgone Accumulators 174

Orgone Cloudbuster. 177-179

pain. 51, 53, 54, 69, 73, 97

Pascual Jordan 182

peer reviewed. 118

pendant 40-43, 47, 48, 51, 52, 57, 59, 62,

63, 67, 70, 74, 75, 78, 80, 82, 94, 97, 102,103,104,105, 107, 108,

135, 149, 150, 151, 194, 198, 203

Periodic Chart of Elements. 208

Peter the Great. 14

Pet Stories. 102

Petrovsky Shungite. 10,147

Phenol. 130

pineal gland. 55

plastic. 126

poison ivy 88

powder in health products. 152

power of intention. 97

produce. 53, 61, 79, 92, 239

Proto-energy. 6, 20, 182, 224

pyramid. 36, 37, 65, 91, 92, 99, 137, 204, 214, 154,

pyrite. 11, 115, 116, 117

Quantum Field. 20, 25, 32, 36, 40, 121, 122,

124, 150, 153, **182**, 185, 193, 194, 195

quartzite. 117

Rabbit Hole. 2, 246

radionics. 130

Raw Shungite. **10,** 20, 69, 93, 100, 114, 115,

123, 126, 133, 150, 151, 153, 194

real Shungite. 10, 101

recharge. 11, 118, 119

red yeast 105

refrigerator magnet, refrigerator. 37, 60, 140

Reiki. 42, 167

renal disease. 106

resonance 124, 125, **169-170,** 173, 175, 199, 210, 229

resin. 33, 118, 153, 194, 203

rheumatoid arthritis. 49

Rife, Dr. Raymond Royal 172-175, 179, 184, 210

Reich, Dr. Wilhelm 149, **174-175,** 177-179, 184, 2019

Rod Huff. 142

rotation............ 20, 22, 28, 111, 130, 137, 161, **187-188**, 190, 240

rust.. 109, 115, 133

S4 magnets............................... 35, 85, 139, 139, 204

S4 powder...................................... 32, 151, 203

S4 Shungite Resin Pendants............................. 41

S4 Sticker............... 73, 80, 81, 86, 93, 108, 134, 135, 136, 139,

Samuel Hahnemann...................................... 168

scar tissue.. 54, 77, 90

shower... 53, 93, 151,

Shunga... 113

Shungite Bees, Shungite Beehives............ 45, 225, 236-241, 244

Shungite Energized Water...................... 13, 123, 126, 131,

132, 145, 152, 156, 158

Shungite environment..................... 38, 45, 62, 76, 77, 104,

108, 150, 158, 236, 241

Shungite Field....... **124,** 132, 139, 140, 142, 147, 152, 187, 191, 205

Shungite Grid.. 123, 158

Shungite Is Used For...................................... 117

Shungite paint....................................... 138, 140

Shungite paneled rooms................................. 14

Shungite Science................................. 20, 163, 183

Shungite Test....................................... 11, 119

Shungite Water...... **13**, 14, 15, 22, 46, 49, 52, 69, 70, 78, 82, 86, 89,

Shungite Reality

90, 102, 104, 105, 106, 107, **117, 123**, 125, 127, 129, 183.

Shungite Weave... 143

Shungite World Grid................................. 123, 143, 242

side effects.. 159

silver saturated... 191-194

silver/gold streaks.. 115

Sixth Extinction Event............................... 225, 227-228

sleep, sleeping better............... 51, 53, 60, 69, 75, 78, 85, 149

smart meter....................................... 33, 62, 84, 136

Smart Sticker................................. 33, 62, 85, 99, **136**

Sofiya Blank....................................... 122, 157, 207

soil............................... 1, 4, 121-122, 144-145, 242

Specific Absorption Rate...................................... 136

stress... 74, 78, 166

Structured Shungite Pendant................................... 42

subtle body.. 165

sulfur, sulfur dioxide gas.................................. 98-99

surgery... 115, 116

swimming pools.. 118, 128

Sympathetic Resonance.................... 124, 125, **169-170,** 173, 175, 199, 210, 229

Tesla, Nikola........................... 157, 175-176, 180, 206

testimonials... 45-112

258

thermography.. 134

thinking clearer... 49

three nuggets 73, 78, 83, 93, 108, **122**,

126, 130, 131, 139, 152, 157, 158, 207

thyroid disease... 49

ticks... 45, 88

torsion field 36, 140, 153, 155, **204-205**

toxic molecule **22, 121, 161**, 189

trembling.. 107

Tsirpursky, Dr. Semeon J............................... 9, 197

tumor.. 78, 89, 106, 212

Twin Towers 9/11 177

types of Shungite...................................... **10, 114**

Universe of Spiritual Intervention........................... **163**

vacuum... 20

vegetables freezing, vegetables...................... 37, 140, 154

Vibrational Medicine............................. **163-164**, 170

vital energy.. 166

Walt Silva... 183

warts... 107

water distiller 109

water heater 26, 73, 125, 128, 156

water molecules .... 126, 25 water purification. **12,** 91, 117, 133

water softener. 109

water system 22, 25, 125, 127

Water Turtle. 129-130

water wells 128

Where Is Shungite Found?.. 7

WiFi. . . . 17-19, 30, **32-35**, 41, 43, 46, 51, 52, 57, 60, 62, 67, 69, 74, 78,

80, 93, 103, 104, 137, 139, 150, 191, **194, 227-236**

Wire-wrapped Pendants.. 40

wound.. . . . . 103, 153

wrist injury. 93

Zazhoginsky.. . . . . 12, 113

ABOUT THE AUTHOR

As a US Army Intelligence Officer, Nancy L. Hopkins was trained in concepts of the "Electronic Battlefield" and "Electronic Warfare", where EMF and WiFi frequencies are critical components to war. It took decades for her to realize Electronic Warfare was also being conducted on the US civilian population.

From spying on everyone to attacking the population energetically with the telecommunication network - there has been a silent, invisible weapon unleashed by the Financial/Industrial Complex that is either doing it with purpose or just does not care about the health consequence of their actions.

End result is the same - The Sixth Extinction Event. Oh, except for a gift called Shungite. Shungite has leveled the playing field giving us the ability to fight back and usher in a new reality.

This book, *Shungite Reality*, relates Nancy's journey to understand the seemingly magical Shungite and to use Shungite to save the bees and all other insects to stop the total collapse of civilization.

Nancy Hopkins is a researcher, author, internet radio host, producer and owner of Cosmic Reality Radio. This is a long road from a 15 year old who saw the reality of her childhood evaporate in an instant with the assassination of President John Kennedy in 1963. Since then, Nancy has been unraveling the tapestry of the reality we have come to know of as The Matrix Reality.

Nancy's book *Cosmic Reality* summarizes that Matrix Reality. Her fiction-based-on-fact book *the 911 Crusade* introduced her to an entirely new level of the Matrix where exotic weapons can cause a 110 story building to turn to dust. The Matrix is a perfect reality. It works just as intended. It was intended to control humanity. You cannot change a perfect reality. You can only build a new reality.

A new reality is built by changing the Collective Consciousness of Humanity. The change comes when enough people believe in the new reality. Internet Radio is an opportunity for individuals to come together to talk and think about all versions of all realities. Change the Collective Consciousness and we will change reality, simply because reality is what we think it is.

You can participate by listening to Cosmic Reality Radio at CosmicReality.com and YouTube station "Cosmic Reality".

The following links may be helpful:

Shungite Store & Information - www.cosmicreality.net

Shungite Beehives Forum - www.shungitebeehives.com

FACE BOOK GROUPS:

"Shungite Reality"

"Cosmic Reality"

"Shungite Beehives"

Made in the USA
Monee, IL
19 June 2020